TUBETEASERS

Also by BRUCE NASH:

The Official Superman Quizbook
The Star Trek Make-a-Game Book
Whatever Happened to Blue Suede Shoes?
The World Championship Boxing Quizbook
The Book of Tests
The Elvis Presley Quizbook
Pundles
Pundles #2
Challenger Pundles
Challenger Pundles #2
Thirty Years of Television
So, You Think You Know Your Girlfriend/Boyfriend?
So, You Think You Know Your Parents?
So, You Think You Know Your Best Friend?
So, You Think You Know Your Brother/Sister?
The Fifties Nostalgia Quizbook
Computer Sports Matchups
The Thumbs Up, Thumbs Down Book of Puns
Can I Quote You on That?
Limer-Wrecks

TUBE TEASERS

TEASERS

THE TV NOSTALGIA QUIZ & PUZZLE BOOK

BRUCE NASH

Contemporary Books, Inc.
chicago

Library of Congress Cataloging in Publication Data

Nash, Bruce M.

  Tubeteasers: the TV nostalgia quiz and puzzle book.
  Reprint. Originally published: South Brunswick, N.J.: A. S. Barnes, 1979.
  1. Television programs — United States — Miscellanea.
I. Title.
[PN1992.9.N32   1984]   791.45'076   83-27309
ISBN 0-8092-5425-5

First Contemporary trade paperback edition 1984

Published by Contemporary Books, Inc.
180 North Michigan Avenue, Chicago, Illinois 60601
Manufactured in the United States of America
Library of Congress Catalog Card Number: 83-27309
International Standard Book Number: 0-8092-5425-5

Published simultaneously in Canada by Beaverbooks, Ltd.
195 Allstate Parkway, Valleywood Business Park
Markham, Ontario L3R 4T8 Canada

To Gug and Eep

Contents

Acknowledgments

Special thanks to my brother, Greg Nash, for his excellent graphic work on the crossword puzzles included in this book.

Photo Credits

All photos used in this book are courtesy of the following corporations and individuals: Worldvision Enterprises, Inc.; © Hanna-Barbera Productions, Inc.; Bob Smith; CBS; Wrather Corporation; Maury Foldare & Associates; Greenway Productions; © P.A.T.—Ward; Richard Webb Productions; National Telefilm Associates, Inc.; Hugh O'Brian; Ivan Tors Films, Inc. and Heritage Enterprises Inc.; George Gobel; Ralph Edwards Productions; Four Star Entertainment Corporation; and Telewide Systems, Inc.

All animated characters included in the Hanna-Barbera photos were created by Hanna-Barbera Productions.

When the Moon Comes Over the Mountain... It's Howdy Doody Time!

Scoop . . . bubble gum cards . . . ice cream cones with chocolate sprinkles . . . button candy . . . Ebbets Field . . . flavor straws . . . bobby sox . . . Dixie Cup lids with movie stars' pictures . . . pompadours . . . Jujubes . . . 3-D movies . . . shoe fluoroscopes . . . and, through it all, there was television. That once curious-looking cabinet with the luminous postage stamp-sized screen was the glue that held these now-nostalgic remembrances together. Television provided the continuity to this kaleidoscope of fads, foibles, and fashions, capturing the mood of the nation and mirroring the country's philosophy, values, frailties, fears, and ideals in its program content. Remembering television is to recall far more than our favorite stars or shows—it is to remember America herself as she once was—strong, united, proud, and content. We look back, reminisce, feel nostalgic, and sadly lament the harsh reality that the good old days are no more.

Unlike other nostalgia quizbooks on the market today, *Tubeteasers* is not a sterile recapitulation of cold facts and figures culled from the dusty archives of television minutiae. It is instead a personal tribute to a medium that has entertained, educated, informed, and enriched the lives of millions of Americans for more than thirty years. Through a combination of questions-and-answers, crossword puzzles, find-a-word games, and photo quizzes, this unique book will take you on a nostalgic sojourn back into that memorable golden era of television programming gone by. For a brief sentimental interlude, time will stand still as all the real and imaginary characters from Television Past come alive once more to rekindle the fond memories that endeared them to our hearts. You will "see" and "hear" their familiar faces and voices once again in a panoramic re-creation of thirty wondrous years of laughter, drama, song, mystery, suspense, pathos—and a lifetime of memories . . . Hi ho,

Steverino! . . . One of these days, Alice—Pow! Right in the kisser! . . . Say, kids! What time is it? . . . Sorry about that, Chief! . . . Our next millionaire, Mike . . . Hey, Wild Bill! Wait for me! . . . Who was that masked man? . . . Ten-four . . . Yabba dabba doo! . . . Say the secret word and you win a hundred dollars . . . Hey, Cisco!—Hey, Pancho! . . . Goodnight, Mrs. Calabash, wherever you are . . . Holy mackerel, Sapphire! . . . You're a real doozy, Mr. B. . . . Yo ho, Rinty! . . . Hey, Abbott! . . . You rang? . . . The Gillette Cavalcade of Sports is on the air! . . . Tonight, right here on our stage . . . What a revoltin' development this is! . . . Just the facts, ma'am . . . Come in Mystery Challenger and sign in please! . . . Yoo hoo! Mrs. Bloom! . . . Tell ya what I'm gonna do! . . . How sweet it is! . . . Thanks for the memories. . . .

Yes, we have developed many vicarious friendships through the intimacy of this electronic medium called television. Fictional characters conjured up in a television writer's idle daydreams shared our living rooms with us week after week as if part of our own family. Many of their voices have been stilled now (save for reruns of programs of more recent vintage)—Chester A. Riley, Hoss Cartwright, Fred Mertz, Major Seth Adams, "Gramps" Miller, Lily Ruskin, Jarrod Barkley, Sergeant Vince Carter, Grandpappy Amos McCoy, Mr. Peepers, Captain Binghamton, Kate Bradley, Hopalong Cassidy. But they will live forever in the memories of those of us who knew and loved them. And so, just for a moment, let us return to those carefree, innocent days of yesteryear . . . to an era without rampant inflation, dope, crippling gas and energy shortages, tight money, war, racial strife, and government corruption . . . to a time in our lives when America laughed and played and took pride in itself . . . the Lone Ranger rides again!

TUBETEASERS

And a-w-a-a-y we go!...

"The Abbott and Costello Show"

Answers on page 173

(1952–54)

1. Before each episode of the show began, Abbott and Costello performed an abbreviated stand-up comedy routine before a howling audience. Probably their most famous sketch dealt with the confusing lineup of a fictitious baseball team. What was the name of this classic comedy routine?

2. In what film did the boys first introduce this sidesplitting comedy bit?

3. The show's theme song, _____, was played over an opening montage of film clips from the comedy team's uproarious motion pictures.

4. What were Abbott and Costello's character names in the series?

5. Bud and Lou portrayed unemployed _____ trying to scrape together enough money to pay their rent by performing odd jobs.

6. The boys lived in a boardinghouse that was run by a bald-headed landlord who was usually seen chewing on a cigar. What was the name of the slovenly attired resident manager who was always feuding with Bud and Lou?

7. Costello was often accosted outside his boardinghouse by a man-sized schoolboy outfitted in a Little Lord Fauntleroy suit. What was the name of Lou's tubby neighborhood nemesis?

8. Which former member of The Three Stooges comedy team appeared in the role of this nasty youngster?

9. The love of the dumpy Costello's life was his across-the-hall neighbor in the boardinghouse. What was the name of Lou's dream girl?

10. Whenever the slapstick duo ran afoul of the law, they were sternly reprimanded by _____ the Cop, the neighborhood constable who often stopped by the boardinghouse while walking his beat.

11. What was the name of the boys' mustachioed Italian friend who kept turning up in a different job in each episode?

12. What type of hat did Lou always wear?

13. What was the name of Lou's pet chimpanzee?

14. What was so unusual about the way his pet chimp dressed?

15. What was Lou's classic expression of self-admonition whenever he had done something naughty?

"The Amos 'n' Andy Show"

Answers on pages 173–74

(1951–53)

1. Although his name did not appear in the show's title, master-schemer George Stevens was the featured character in this vintage ethnic comedy. What was the fishy-sounding nickname of this con artist who was always trying to sucker poor, unsuspecting Andy into one of his shady deals?

2. What was the slow-thinking Andy's last name?

3. What was his nickname?

4. Holy mackerel! Mrs. Stevens frequently chided her husband for being a shiftless, good-for-nothing loafer. What was the first name of this shrewish woman?

5. Stevens hatched most of his money-making schemes from his "office" at the neighborhood lodge hall. What was the name of the meeting place that served as the locale for most of the comedy action in the series?

6. The slow-moving janitor who cleaned up around the lodge hall was ironically nicknamed _____.

7. Amos Jones was an honest, soft-spoken hack who drove the only cab in the _____ Taxi Cab Company of America's fleet.

8. What was the name of the hard-working cabbie's wife?

9. Who was the president of the cab company?

10. What was the name of the cab company's secretary?

11. In what city did the comedy series take place?

12. Chewing on his familiar cigar stub, Andy often daydreamed about his true love, the widow Madame _____.

13. What was the Madame's line of work?

14. What was the name of the boys' shyster lawyer?

15. What was the title of the series' popular theme song?

"The Andy Griffith Show"

Answers on page 174–75

(1960–68)

1. Andy Griffith brought his own brand of corn pone humor to television in this situation comedy about country life in a rural North Carolina community. In the series, Andy portrayed the town's mild-mannered sheriff who maintained the local peace without having to carry a gun. What was the name of the homespun law enforcement officer he played?

2. Aside from doing the local sheriffing, what other town chores did Andy handle during the early days of the series?

3. What was the name of the sheriff's young, freckle-faced son?

4. Living with the widower sheriff and his carrot-topped son was their motherly Aunt _____, a gentle woman who prided herself on her culinary skills.

5. Originally cast as townie Henrietta Perkins in the show's pilot episode, _____ swapped aprons and kitchens to create the recurring role of Andy's good-natured aunt.

6. The setting of "The Andy Griffith Show" was the sleepy hamlet of _____, North Carolina.

7. What was the name of Andy's overzealous deputy?

8. Fragile-looking _____ appeared as the town's junior lawman.

9. For fear of accidentally shooting himself or an innocent bystander, Andy's clumsy deputy never carried a loaded gun. He did, however, keep a single round of ammunition close by for use in times of dire emergency. Where did the gun-shy officer keep this lone bullet hidden?

10. What was the name of the high-strung deputy's steady girl friend?

11. What was her three-digit telephone number?

12. What was the name of the impulsive deputy's landlady?

13. What was the name of the overbearing constable who became Andy's new deputy after his longtime assistant departed for Raleigh?

14. Andy's first girl friend in the series worked for her Uncle Fred in the neighborhood drugstore. What was the name of the former teenage co-star of "Father Knows Best" who grew up to portray the folksy sheriff's sweetheart, Ellie Walker?

15. The local barber shop served as a meeting place for the sharing of the latest town gossip. What was the name of the scatterbrained busybody who owned the barber salon?

16. What was the name of the pretty blond-haired nurse whom Andy dated steadily for a spell?

17. Before he bade his friends goodbye and departed for a tour of active duty in the Marine Corps, Gomer Pyle worked as a local service station attendant. What is the name of the singer-comedian who portrayed Andy's good-natured friend?

18. What was the first name of the owner of the filling station where Gomer worked?

19. After Gomer's induction into the Armed Forces, his pea-brained cousin became the town's resident grease-monkey. What was the name of this sappy-looking country bumpkin with the crown-shaped cap?

20. What was the name of his blonde girlfriend who worked at the local diner?

21. Forced to cater to his overprotective mother's every wish, straight-laced county clerk _____ found little time to enjoy a normal social life.

22. Formerly the mother of "Bewitched" hubby Darrin Stevens, _____ appeared as the clerk's hypochondriac mother.

23. Always trying to keep pace with his younger companions, middle-aged _____ operated the local fix-it shop.

24. What was the name of the appliance repairman's loving wife?

25. Always critical of Sheriff Andy's methods of operation was town Mayor _____.

26. The original Chester Goode in "Gunsmoke" 's early radio days, _____ made infrequent appearances as the municipality's obnoxious chief official.

27. Who had been his predecessor as mayor of the rural community in the early days of the series?

28. Who was the proprietor of the local department store?

29. Long before she began dating town councilman Sam Jones on "Mayberry R.F.D.," Millie Swanson kept company with one of Andy's pals. Which one?

30. What was the name of the bakery where Millie dispensed cream puffs and rum cakes?

31. Andy married his favorite girl in the series' final year on television. What was the name of the schoolteacher who became the sheriff's blushing bride?

32. What grade did she teach in school?

33. The cell door of the jailhouse was always kept unlocked for the town drunk's regular Saturday night visit. What was the name of the happy-go-lucky sot who spent most of his weekends sleeping off a hangover in Andy's jail?

34. How many "maximum-security" cells were located in Andy's jail?

35. What was the name of the local operator who assisted townfolk in placing their telephone calls?

36. Semiliterate Ernest T. Bass continued to court hillbilly lovely Charlene Darling even though she had already married Dud Walsh. Spurned by his heartthrob and reprimanded by Andy for pursuing Charlene's affections, Ernest acted out his frustrations by throwing rocks through neighbors' windows. What former regular on Sid Caesar's "Your Show of Shows" appeared as this headstrong and lovesick yokel?

37. _____ Lake was the scene of many picnics and family outings for Andy and his friends.

38. Local townfolk often drove over to the county seat of Mt. _____ to seek "big city" shopping, restaurants, and other forms of entertainment.

39. What was the most popular eatin' place in town (aside from Aunt Bee's kitchen, that is)?

40. The "good ol' boys" on this prize-winning rural sitcom were originally introduced to television viewers in a pilot episode on comedian _____'s popular weekly series.

Action, Thrills, and High Adventure!

Answers on page 175

Find the names of the following characters and personalities from adventure programs in the maze of alphabet jibberish:

1. Sergeant Preston's "swiftest and strongest lead dog"
2. Skipper Adam Troy's "Adventures in Paradise" schooner
3. "Jungle Jim" 's pet chimpanzee
4. "Riverboat" pilot Dan Frazer
5. "It Takes a Thief" 's cat burglar-turned-undercover spy
6. Jim Sinclair, modern-day "Cowboy in Africa"
7. Robert Shaw's "Buccaneers" role
8. The Bedloes' 600-pound pacifist bear
9. "Crunch and Des" 's charter boat
10. "Rescue 8" paramedic Wes Cameron
11. "Mr. Lucky" 's gambling partner
12. "Foreign Legionnaire" Captain Gallant's ward
13. "Daktari" 's cross-eyed lion
14. "Sea Hunt" 's aquatic adventurer, Mike Nelson
15. "Route 66" wanderer Tod Stiles
16. Soldier of fortune "China Smith"
17. Daniel Boone's Oxford-educated Indian sidekick
18. Sandy and Bud Rick's pet dolphin
19. Jungle doctor Tom Reynolds's African title
20. Dying attorney who "ran for his life" after doctor told him he only had two years to live

Courtesy Greenway Productions

Courtesy Greenway Productions.

Courtesy Greenway Productions.

5. Often stymied by the city's criminal masterminds, Police Commissioner _____ relied upon Batman and Robin to bring these resourceful crooks to justice.

6. Who was Gotham City's venerable Chief of Police?

7. The Batgirl frequently assisted Batman and Robin in maintaining the peace in Gotham City. What was the Batgirl's secret identity?

8. What vehicle did Batgirl use to track down criminals?

9. Match the Caped Crusader's villainous foe with the actor who portrayed him:

The Penguin	Walter Slezak
King Tut	David Wayne
The Riddler	Cesar Romero
The Mad Hatter	Burgess Meredith
Clock King	Frank Gorshin and John Astin
The Joker	Victor Buono
The Minstrel	Van Johnson
The Bookworm	Art Carney
Archer	Liberace
Chandell	Michael Rennie
The Sandman	Roddy McDowall

10. Famous movie tough guy and Academy Award-winner for his supporting role in *All About Eve*, _____ became the second actor to appear as Batman's arch-enemy, Mr. Freeze, the fiendish criminal who could only survive at fifty degrees below zero.

11. Bam! Pow! Zowie! What was the Riddler's mob of dastardly criminals called?

12. The Mad Hatter was otherwise known as Jervis _____.

13. What was the name of the evil Bat-enemy who deceptively evaded the dynamic duo in his role as the "villainous master of disguise"?

14. Prestidigitator Anne Baxter baffled the Batman with her feats of legerdemain as the magician-turned-jewel thief, _____ the Great.

15. What three performers appeared in the role of Batman's feline arch-nemesis, the Catwoman?

16. What was the name of Batman's aunt?

17. Fill in the missing blanks to describe the following Bat-gadgets:

    The _____ Scanner
    The _____ Batsorter
    The _____ Analyzer
    The _____ Secret Writing Detector

18. What was the source of power for the Batpole?

19. Cartoonist _____ created the comic-book hero who fought crime and injustice in Gotham City.

20. Described by his creator as "just an average millionaire out there fighting master criminals," Batman first appeared on the drawing board as Birdman, a composite super-hero drawn from the likes of Superman, the Green Hornet, Zorro, and the Bat. In what comic book did the Caped Crusader make his first public appearance?

"Ben Casey"

Answers on page 178

(1961–66)

1. What was the name of the actor who starred as Dr. Ben Casey, the snarling, introverted surgeon who was fanatically devoted to his medical career?

2. In what field of medicine did Casey specialize?

3. Charged with the responsibility for tempering Casey's frequent outbreaks of moodiness and impetuosity was the hospital's Chief of Neurosurgery, Dr. _____.

4. Looking as if his hair were standing on end from the charge of an electrical shock, _____ starred as Casey's learned supervisor.

5. This frizzly locked actor's real-life wife, Bettye Ackerman, appeared as the brooding Casey's romantic interest in the series. What was the name of the staff physician she portrayed?

6. What position did the surly physician's girl friend occupy in the hospital?

7. Lover of food, drink, and women, divorced physician _____ came from a well-to-do family and possessed all the attributes of success—money, a sparkling personality, and good looks.

8. During the summer of 1965, Dr. David _____ arrived on the scene, sporting a well-groomed beard, as the hospital's new Chief of Neurosurgery and Casey's second television boss.

9. What was the name of the distinguished motion picture actor, twice-nominated for an Academy Award for his performances in *Mutiny on the Bounty* and *Lives of a Bengal Lancer*, who portrayed this new member of the cast?

10. What was the name of the hospital that formed the setting for these medical dramas?

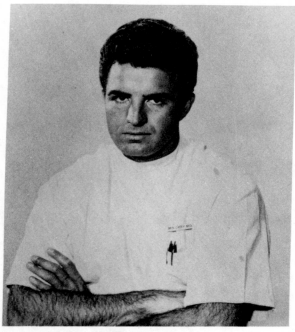

Courtesy Worldvision Enterprises, Inc.

Crossword #1

Photo Courtesy Worldvision Enterprises, Inc.

Answers on page 179

Clues

Across

1. Boris Karloff starred as a one-eyed police Inspector in "_____ _____ _____ Scotland Yard"

11. "The _____ Squad," spy drama starring Bob Hastings

12. "The Door with _____ Name," spy drama set in Washington, D.C.

13. Henry Fonda portrayed Marshal Simon _____ in "The Deputy"

31

15. Type of duty for crew members who misbehaved on "The Wackiest Ship in the Army"
17. "_____ Smith Goes to Washington" cast Fess Parker as a rural politician who becomes a U.S. Senator
19. "M*A*S*H" 's pacifist surgeon, Captain Hawkeye Pierce (initials)
20. The crimes investigated on this dramatic series were murder, kidnapping, and robbery
21. Orson _____, panelist on "To Tell the Truth" and "Laugh Line"
22. Relationship of Steve Douglas to Mike, Robbie, and Chip
23. **PHOTO CLUE:** He played Doc on this World War II dramatic series featuring the exploits of K Company (initials)
25. A small number of units or individuals
26. **PHOTO CLUE:** Rick Jason appeared as the rugged Lt. _____ Hanley
27. Producer Norman Lear's production company
28. Marked by a definite order
29. Gene Lockhart appeared as "_____ Honor, Homer Bell"
30. Marlin Perkins hosted the animal documentary series "_____ Kingdom"
31. "_____ You Positive?," game show in which celebrity panelists tried to guess identity of famous people from their baby pictures
33. "_____ It to the Camera," hosted by Red Rowe and created by Alan Funt
34. Occupation of Fred Baker on "Channing"
35. Joke-telling game series, "Can You _____ This?"
37. "Star _____," enormously popular sci-fi series
38. Early TV charade game, "_____ Lucky"
39. Lionel Morton played the chief agent on this wartime series
41. "The _____ _____ _____ _____," a musical variety series featuring The Randy Van Horne Singers and The Boataneers
44. "Wayne and Shuster Take _____ Affectionate Look At . . .," comedy series
45. _____-star, share equal billing with fellow performer on a TV series
46. Kelly Robinson and Scotty traveled around the world as undercover agents masquerading as a tennis pro and his trainer in "_____ _____"
47. Her alter-ego is schoolteacher Andrea Thomas
48. Fabian appeared on "Bus Stop" in an episode entitled "_____ by an Idiot"

Down

1. "_____," game show on which contestants tried to match like objects and solve a hidden puzzle
2. "_____ _____ _____ _____," prehistoric world inhabited by the Marshall family
3. "Rich Man, Poor Man" 's Nick Nolte's role on "Adams of Eagle Lake" (initials)

4. Major Robert Rogers was in search of the "_____ Passage"
5. "Auntie" on perennial spring telecast, the movie *The Wizard of Oz*
6. "_____ _____ Face," game show in which contestants pieced together puzzle parts of celebrity faces
7. What Shirley Conway was on "The Nurses" (abbreviation)
8. **PHOTO CLUE:** Wartime saga in which pictured infantry soldier starred
9. "Festival _____ Stars," anthology series featuring selected rebroadcasts from "The Loretta Young Theatre"
10. She shared top billing with Don Ameche on a variety series that included excerpts from her diary, *Purple Heart*
14. How Katy Holstrum, "The Farmer's Daughter," would answer "yes" to her congressman-employer, Glen Morley
16. Gene Barry as Gene Talbot taught this subject at "Our Miss Brooks" 's school (abbreviation)
18. Rocky Lane portrayed "_____ Ryder," cowboy hero who teamed with Little Beaver to fight outlaws
24. An oaf
30. Satire adapted from a popular British series, "That Was the _____ That Was"
32. Host of "G.E. College Bowl" (initials)
34. What "Boston Blackie," "Ellery Queen," and "Mannix" did as their job
35. Asta the dog was the "third lead" in the mystery-detective series "The _____ Man"
36. Patti _____'s first TV series was "The Scott Music Hall"
37. What Chester A. Riley worked with at his plant
40. Belonging to Mr. Spade
42. _____ Kyser appeared as "The Old Professor" on his variety-quiz series
43. "Barney Miller" 's Sergeant Yemana

"The Beverly Hillbillies"

Answers on pages 179–80

(1962-71)

1. Buddy Ebsen starred as the itinerant mountaineer who accidentally unearthed crude oil while shooting at wild game. What was the name of the hillbilly patriarch who became an overnight millionaire?

2. With "black gold" oozing out of the Clampett property, joyous kinfolk urged the grizzled Ozarker to depart his squalid surroundings for a life of luxury in Beverly Hills. One member of the hillbilly clan, Granny Clampett, didn't cotton, however, to the idea of forsaking the good mountain life for a more urbane existence. What was the first name of the shotgun-wielding grandma who was begrudgingly transported to California in her rocking chair?

3. What was the name of the oilman who made the Clampetts rich by buying the rights to their oil-drenched land?

4. How many millions of dollars were the Ozarkers paid for their "Texas tea"?

5. In what Ozark town were the Clampetts living at the time they struck it rich?

6. Accompanying the Clampetts to their newly purchased California estate was the prosperous hillbilly clan leader's rock-headed nephew. What was the name of this girl-crazy hayseed?

7. How many years of formal schooling did this backwards Ozarker have?

8. Son of a former heavyweight boxing champion, actor _____ doubled as his piano-playing twin sister, Jethrene.

9. Who supplied the dubbed-in voice of this mountain Amazon?

10. Jethrene and her doting mother stayed behind while the rest of the family embarked on their trip to the West Coast. Formerly a regular on both "The George Burns and Gracie Allen Show" and "Petticoat Junction," Bea Benaderet portrayed the Clampetts' widowed cousin, _____ Bodine.

11. The youngest member of the Clampett family was a curvaceous, blonde-haired mountain gal who surrounded herself with a menagerie of animal friends. What was the name of this critter-lovin' beauty?

12. What was the regal name of the Clampetts' hound dog?

13. What was the address of the Clampetts' palatial Beverly Hills mansion?

14. What was the name of the bank where the Clampetts kept their fortune stored?

15. Banker _____ Drysdale connived and schemed to maintain control over the hillbillies' multimillion-dollar account.

16. Aside from being their banker, Mr. Drysdale lived next door to the Clampetts. Unlike her husband, the status-conscious Mrs. Drysdale was determined to drive the Ozark hillbillies out of her exclusive neighborhood. What was this snooty woman's first name?

17. What was the name of the Drysdales' maid?

18. What was the name of their butler?

19. Comedian _____ made occasional appearances as the Drysdales' "Sonny."

20. How many years did the Drysdales' son spend in college before returning home?

21. Formerly Judge Bradley Stevens in the vintage situation comedy "I Married Joan," _____ appeared as Mr. Drysdale's boss, Martin Van Ranshoff.

22. The greedy Mr. Drysdale's administrative assistant did not approve of her employer's underhanded tactics. What was the name of the homely financial aide who nurtured a burning desire for the affections of the senior Clampett's oafish nephew?

23. The Clampetts entertained dinner guests in their "fancy eatin' room." Where did the transplanted mountain people serve their company victuals?

24. The hillbillies slaughtered the King's English and adopted down-home euphemisms to describe their posh surroundings. What did they call their swimming pool that served as a communal trough for all the family's critters?

25. The banjo-picking duet of Lester _____ and Earl _____ played the country-western theme for the series.

"Bewitched"

Answers on pages 180–81

(1964-72)

1. Darrin Stevens, a mere mortal, led a hectic and often perplexing life being married to a beautiful witch. What two actors starred as this "bewitched" hubby?

2. Who portrayed Darrin's supernaturally endowed wife, Samantha?

3. What was Samantha's nickname?

4. What was the address of the Stevens's home?

5. What was the name of the advertising agency where Darrin worked?

6. Who was Darrin's overbearing and demanding boss?

7. What was the name of his employer's wife?

8. The Stevens' daughter inherited her mother's power of witchcraft. What was their magically imbued offspring's name?

9. What was the name of the couple's mortal son?

10. What was the name of Samantha's opinionated mother?

11. Samantha's mother vehemently disapproved of her daughter's marriage to a mortal. How did she derisively mispronounce Darrin's name?

12. What were the names of Darrin's parents?

13. Samantha's sister was her opposite, dressing in mod clothes, talking in hip lingo, and living the swinging singles life style. What was her name?

14. Who portrayed Samantha's footloose and fancy-free sibling?

15. What was the name of the Stevens' buttinsky neighbor who was always being stymied in her efforts to expose Samantha's witchcraft?

16. What was the name of her disbelieving husband?

17. What was the name of the warlock physician who treated Samantha's side of the family?

18. What was the name of Samantha's bumbling aunt who once caused a thirteen-state blackout on the east coast of the United States when her witchcraft went awry?

19. What veteran comedian appeared as Samantha's warlock Uncle Arthur?

20. How did Samantha conjure up her witchcraft?

"Bonanza"

Answers on page 181

(1959-73)

1. This extremely popular Western series featured the adventurous exploits of a moralistic, Bible-quoting father and his three respectfully obedient sons. What was the name of the gray-haired widower who lorded over a prosperous ranch situated in the heart of the Nevada silver-mining territory?

2. What were the names of this western patriarch's three former wives?

3. What was his occupation before he became a prosperous ranch owner?

4. The Cartwrights' expansive land holdings were located on the outskirts of _____ City.

5. What was the name of the middle-aged sheriff of this frontier city?

6. The Cartwright ranch was a symbol of wealth, power, and prestige to local ranchers. What was the name of their renowned spread?

7. "Haunted" by an earlier role he'd played as a teenage werewolf, _____ starred as the impulsive, hot-tempered Little Joe.

8. _____ created the memorable role of the gentle behemoth, "Hoss," fun-loving and soft-spoken middle son of the Cartwright clan.

9. Although everyone in town referred to him by his aptly bestowed nickname, Hoss's actual first name was _____.

10. Before departing the series in 1965, Pernell Roberts appeared as the eldest of the three Cartwright sons. What was the biblical name of this pensive, serious-minded offspring?

11. How were the three Cartwright boys actually related?

12. What was the name of the good-natured stray ranch hand who was added to the permanent cast to fill the void created by the absence of the Cartwrights' oldest son?

13. Only one of the Cartwrights drew his pistol with his left hand. Which member of the family had a southpaw trigger-finger?

14. In an attempt to rejuvenate the show's ratings following the real-life/screen death of brother Hoss, a young drifter who had just been released from prison was signed on by the Cartwright family as a new ranch hand. What was this newcomer's name?

15. The Cartwrights' Oriental cook, _____, busied himself by catering to the family's giant-sized appetites.

"Circus Boy"

Answers on pages 181–82

(1956–58)

1. This series featured the dramatic adventures of a turn-of-the-century traveling circus as it roamed from town to town delighting men, women, and children of all ages. What festive event was featured in the opening segment of each episode?

2. Circus Boy's parents were aerialists who were tragically killed in a high-wire accident under the Big Top. What was the name of his parents' act?

3. Orphaned by the sudden death of his aerialist parents, Circus Boy was looked after by a warm-hearted circus clown named_____.

4. Now cast as Jim Rockford's father in the popular NBC series "The Rockford Files,"_____appeared as the orphan boy's clown-friend.

5. What was Circus Boy's first name?

6. From "Circus Boy," he went on to take his place as one of the rock 'n' roll Monkees singing group. Who is this talented performer?

7. What was the name of Circus Boy's inseparable elephant companion?

8. What was the name of the burly boss canvassman whose bark was much worse than his bite?

9. What was the name of the circus's owner?

10. Match the names of the following circus performers with their "Big Top" jobs:

Mamie	Escape artist
Firpo	Lion tamer
Gambino	Wardrobe
Billy Stanton	Veterinarian
Pop Warren	Knife thrower
Ricardo	Trick shooter

"The Dick Van Dyke Show"

Answers on pages 182–83

(1961-66)

1. Dick Van Dyke starred as the head comedy writer of a mythical variety program, "The Alan Brady Show." What was the name of the gangly punster he portrayed?

2. A former host on the early television variety series "Broadway Open House," cello-playing_____delivered an endless succession of one-line quips in his role as comedy staff writer Buddy Sorrell.

3. What was the unusual name of Buddy's infrequently seen spouse?

Courtesy CBS.

4. What did she do for a living before marrying Buddy?

5. Rounding out the trio of gag writers for "The Alan Brady Show" was the husbandless Sally Rogers. What was the name of the blonde-haired comedienne who portrayed her in the series?

6. Although Sally always kept her eyes open for the right guy, she seemed resigned to the fact that she would remain a spinster. What was the name of Sally's frequent date who unfortunately was still tied to his mother's apron strings?

7. The bald-headed producer of "The Alan Brady Show" was constantly reminded of his hairless condition by Buddy's unflattering jokes. A former regular on "Leave It to Beaver" and "The Mothers-in-Law,"_____starred as the dome-topped television executive.

8. What was the name of the bullied "whipping boy" he portrayed in the series?

9. What is the name of the creative genius who played the comedy writers' domineering boss, Alan Brady?

10. Alan Brady always lamented the fact that he and the show's exasperating producer were related. Exactly what was the relationship between these two men?

11. What was the name of the switchboard operator at the offices of "The Alan Brady Show"?

12. Featured in an earlier role as the legs of the otherwise-unseen switchboard girl "Sam" on "Richard Diamond, Private Eye," _____ played the role of Dick Van Dyke's wife, Laura.

13. What was Laura's maiden name?

14. What was the name of the couple's son?

15. Not wanting to offend any family member who had suggested a middle name for their baby son, Rob and Laura derived a unique solution to their ticklish problem. Taking the first letter of each name proposed, the young couple arrived at the family-pleasing yet odd Wellesian acronym, "_____."

16. Rob first met his bride-to-be while a serviceman stationed at Camp _____.

17. What rank did Rob hold in the Special Services Division of the Army?

18. What was Laura's occupation at the time her courtship with Rob began?

19. Rob broke up his hometown engagement to marry Laura while on a three-day pass. What was the name of the fiancée he ditched?

20. What was the name of Rob's loud-mouthed service buddy who had a knack for intruding upon his and Laura's privacy?

21. In what eastern city did the Petries live?

22. What was their street address?

23. The Petries' closest friends and next-door neighbors were _____ and _____ Halper.

24. What was Mr. Halper's professional calling?

25. Aside from his portrayal of the Petries' next-door friend, talented Jerry Paris handled additional chores as the series' _____.

26. The Halpers' son, _____, was often next door playing with his best friend, the Petries' boy.

27. J. Pat O'Malley and Isabel Randolph infrequently appeared as Rob's parents. What were their first names?

28. Rob's introverted brother was a no-talent stick-in-the-mud who was miraculously transformed into a live-wire, banjo-pickin' entertainer whenever he walked in his sleep. What was the name of this Jekyll-Hyde somnambulist?

29. Who portrayed him in the series?

30. The last episode to be filmed in the series' five-year history was a spoof of a well-known western film. The only installment of the series to be shot entirely on location, "The Gunslinger" was a hilarious parody of the motion picture classic _____.

"Dr. Kildare"

Answers on page 183

(1961-66)

1. What is the name of the handsome Shakespearean actor who brought the Dr. Kildare character to life on television?

2. What distinguished actor had previously appeared as the young doctor in the popular movie series?

3. Introduced to television viewers in 1961 as an inexperienced intern, the innocent Kildare matured into a seasoned resident by series' end. What was the boyish-looking doctor's first name?

4. The hospital's Chief of Staff molded the aspiring medical novice into a skilled practitioner. What veteran actor starred as Kildare's understanding mentor?

5. What was the name of the medical supervisor he portrayed in the series?

6. After arriving at the hospital as the new Director of Nurses, Veronica _____ quickly became romantically interested in Kildare's aging boss.

7. What was the name of the veteran film star who portrayed the new chief nurse?

8. Lee Kurty appeared as Nurse Zoe _____, Kildare's romantic flame in the series.

9. During the program's five-year run on television, every malady from hypochondria to brain tumors was treated by the staff of _____ General Hospital.

10. What was the title of the theme song from this medical drama?

Laugh-Riot

Answers on page 183

Find the names of the following characters and personalities from situation comedies in the maze of alphabet jibberish:

1. Patriarch of "The Brady Bunch" clan
2. Dick Van Dyke's second TV missus
3. "My Friend Irma" 's landlady
4. "The Odd Couple" 's poker-playing policeman-friend
5. Phoebe Figalilly's more familiar title
6. "The Real McCoy" 's Grandpappy Amos
7. Principal at "Our Miss Brooks" 's Madison High School
8. "The Munsters" ' pet bat
9. "Maude" 's original maid
10. Herb and Eve on "The Mothers-in-Law"
11. "Private Secretary"—Susie McNamara
12. "The Happy Homemaker" on "The Mary Tyler Moore Show"
13. First commanding officer of the 4077th "M*A*S*H" unit
14. "The Partridge Family" 's manager
15. Landlord on "Wendy and Me"
16. Lucy Carmichael's banker-boss on "Here's Lucy"
17. Proprietress of "Petticoat Junction" 's Shady Rest Hotel
18. "Please Don't Eat the Daisies" family
19. Skipper of P.T. Boat 73
20. Beautiful female robot on "My Living Doll"

```
S N A N N E R B B U R N S H Y
H O D A K O G E A L E E T U E
U K O W A B O E L E G N A L D
C Y L I T E L V M Y O N I A D
R A I F E A G A I A D O H R E
O R J A H Y E N K L U R A S F
D R U C O S A Y E E W B I A F
O U M I N N I N A R B O G L E
S M A G N O N A C U L T O A N
O A V Y E A Y I H T A R R N I
T H Y O E S S U A R I S A U L
H A S U N N O H B D D U V E K
E T S C Y O O Y A I Y S E N N
R E U B E N S O Y L L I E R O
N E T O R E H E M O K E R O C
```

"The Donna Reed Show"

Answers on page 184

(1958–66)

1. What was the last name of America's number-one purity-and-goodness television family?
2. In what city did Donna and her brood live?

3. Donna's husband maintained his business office in the rear of the family's home. What type of work did he do?

4. What was his name?

5. Following his portrayal as Donna's spouse, _____ created the role of a high-powered Texas attorney in the short-lived dramatic series "Judd for the Defense."

6. When she wasn't embroiled in an argument with her younger brother, the couple's snobby teenage daughter was thinking up ways to enhance her popularity at school. What was the name of this boy-crazy social climber?

7. Accorded critical acclaim for her role in the enormously successful made-for-television movie *Brian's Song*, and formerly co-starring opposite Brian Keith in the popular comedy series "The Little People," _____ appeared as this stuck-up adolescent status-seeker.

8. What was the name of the pop record she cut while still a child star on this ultra-wholesome family comedy?

9. Badgered by his sister's endless barrage of put-me-downs was her younger brother, _____.

10. Following his portrayal as this harassed offspring, _____ enjoyed a brief musical career with his recording of the hit song "My Dad."

11. What was the name of the family's "adopted" daughter who first entered their lives by following them home from a picnic one day?

12. What was the name of the family's wisecracking pediatrician-neighbor?

13. Veteran situation-comedy star _____ is often forgotten for his early role as the family's next-door neighbor.

14. What was the first name of the next-door neighbor's wife?

15. Amanda and Bull _____ were the original owners of Donna's quaint home.

Crossword #2

Photo Courtesy Worldvision Enterprises, Inc.

Answers on page 185

Clues

Across

1. **PHOTO CLUE:** Once a female regular on the celebrated pianist's musical variety series

6. The "lonesome" comedian

12. "_____ Common," 1954 game show hosted by Ralph Story

13. "_____ 222," classroom comedy-drama set in Walt Whitman High School

15. Real surname of cowboy star Roy Rogers
16. The go-go dancing "Girl in the Cage" on "Hullabaloo" (initials)
17. Edgar Buchanan starred as this frontier judge
19. What "Secret Squirrel" or "Rocky" might eat
21. Rank of Gomer Pyle's Marine Corps superior, Vince Carter
23. Rosemary _____ played daughter Katrin Hanson on "I Remember Mama"
25. Dean Jones created the role of "_____ O'Toole" in a Navy sitcom
27. John Neville played this lead role in a famous Shakespearean play broadcast in 1957
28. She played Archie Bunker's dingbat spouse
29. "_____ This Is Hollywood," situation comedy starring Mitzi Green
30. Dread or terror
32. Relationship of John Morton to "Mr: Roberts" (abbreviation)
34. "Dough _____ Mi," musical game show hosted by Gene Rayburn
35. She played Bing Crosby's younger daughter, Janice Collins, in the crooner's only TV sitcom
36. Fragrant compound formed by the reaction of alcohol and acid
38. Julie Fielding's mother on "Follow Your Heart" (initials)
39. Ray's partner on "Club Embassy"
40. Art Baker and Jack Smith provided viewers with what they wanted to see on "_____ Asked For It"
42. Arlene Francis hosted this daily women's television magazine
43. _____ Story, host of "The $64,000 Challenge"
45. Buster Crabbe starred as "_____ Gallant of the Foreign Legion"
51. The Louds were the subject of "_____ American Family"
52. **PHOTO CLUE:** Bongo player extraordinary on the sequin-studded entertainer's musical variety series
53. Sid Caesar's distaff comedy team partner (initials)
55. "_____ Your Account," game show in which the neediest contestants received cash
56. John Nagy's TV specialty
57. He co-starred with Jane Powell in the video presentation of "Meet Me in St. Louis" (initials)
58. John Forsythe appeared as Professor Michael Endicott in "_____ Rome With Love"
59. Art Linkletter's segment "_____ Say The Darndest Things"
62. Mrs. Hubbard on "The Mothers-in-Law"
64. He starred opposite Private Hal March on "The Soldiers" (initials)
65. _____ Burke, millionaire police captain of the Metropolitan Homicide Squad
66. "_____ _____!," sitcom featuring Jeannie Carson as a Scottish immigrant trying to adjust to an American life style

Down

1. **PHOTO CLUE:** The pictured maestro himself
2. "_____ Woman's Experience," early DuMont series featuring human interest tales
3. "Pea picker" Tennessee _____ Ford, musical variety series host
4. He co-starred wtih Sir Ralph Richardson in a three-hour telecast of *Richard III* on "Wide Wide World" in 1956 (initials)
5. Private detective Michael Lanyard, the "_____ Wolf"
7. The host of "Official Detective" (initials)
8. He co-hosted "Kids and Company" with cartoonist Ham Fisher
9. John Randolph on the soaper "Another World"
10. Max Liebman presented the music of this famous composer in an early TV special starring Cab Calloway, Ethel Merman, Tony Bennett, and many others
11. George Burns appeared as himself in the situation comedy "Wendy and _____"
14. The skipper of "Tugboat Annie" (initials)
16. Dancer Cyd Charisse has great ones
18. Russell _____, original cast member of "Your Hit Parade"
20. "_____ Cat," featuring Thomas Hewitt Edward as Robert Loggin, cat burglar-turned-bodyguard
22. Occupation of Ernest Bilko's stooges
24. Harold Huber starred as New York columnist Johnny Warren in "I_____ Times Square"
26. Number of children "The Thin Man" and his wife, Nora, had
30. Darrin Stevens on "Bewitched" designed one as part of his job
31. Goodman and Jane were the husband-wife comedy team in "_____ Aces"
33. Cadet Happy, co-pilot on "Space Patrol"
34. Johnny Cash sung the theme song for the Western "The _____"
37. Tony Musante's role as an undercover cop
41. "_____ to Paar," variety series
44. Mary Martin starred in the "Producers' Showcase" version of "Peter _____"
45. Co-star of "The 77th Bengal Lancers"
46. _____ Fleming, long-time host of "Jeopardy"
47. 3.14
48. _____ Hunter was lovey-dovey with Jane Powell in the TV production of "Meet Me in St. Louis"
49. Patriarch Gomez of "The Addams Family"
50. Bruce Gordon played gangland Boss Frank _____ on "The Untouchables"
51. Singer-composer who used to appear frequently on "American Bandstand"

52. He was "At Large" in his first television series
54. "_____ Three," crime drama starring Richard Travis as Sheriff Barrett
55. "_____," World War II series starring Ron Randall as Intelligence Agent Frank Hawthorn
60. "_____ the Law," starring George Raft
61. Dave Willock and Cliff Arquette co-starred on the hobby show "_____-It-Yourself"
62. He portrayed Sundance on "Hotel de Paree" (initials)
63. "Ukulele Ike" on early variety series (initials)

"Dragnet"

Answers on pages 185–86

(1952–70)

1. Dum, Da-Dum-Dum! Straightforward in his interrogation of both witnesses and suspects and unflinching in his pursuit of dangerous lawbreakers, _____ starred each week as Sergeant Joe Friday.
2. Who was Sgt. Friday's first partner?
3. After becoming Friday's partner during the series' second season, Officer _____ continued to serve with him for the next seven years.
4. What was the name of the pudgy ex-silent screen actor who portrayed Friday's long-time partner?
5. Ardent viewers of this hard-hitting crime drama will never forget what took place shortly before the series departed the airwaves for the first time in 1959. What happened in this great moment in television history?
6. After a long, successful run on prime-time television, "Dragnet" moved into syndication renamed "Badge _____," Friday's police identification number.
7. When "Dragnet" resurfaced as a weekly prime-time series in the late sixties, Friday had taken on a new sidekick. What was the name of the former "Pete and Gladys" star who formed the other half of this crime-fighting duo?
8. What was the name of the police officer he portrayed?
9. What was the name of Sgt. Friday's one-time fiancée?

10. "Dragnet" featured factually based stories taken from the files of the _____ Police Department.

11. What was the name of the famous unseen announcer on this cops-and-robbers classic?

12. After a case was wrapped up, the audience was informed that the story they had just seen was true—the names had been changed to _____.

13. What information was provided in the epilogue to each episode?

14. At the conclusion of each episode, the audience watched the perspiring arms of a muscular blacksmith pound a mallet into a die marker to identify the program as a _____ Production.

15. How many times did the faceless smithy strike the mallet before upraising it to reveal the name of the production company?

"The Ed Sullivan Show"

Answers on pages 186–87

(1948-71)

1. What was the original name of Ed Sullivan's weekly variety hour?

2. Always promising a "really big shew," Ed introduced many rising stars to his Sunday-night television audiences. Before gravitating to the small screen, Sullivan worked as a sportswriter and Broadway columnist for a major metropolitan newspaper. Which one?

3. What was the name of the chorus of dancing girls who appeared as regular members of the original Sullivan show troupe?

4. What do singing fireman John Kokoman, pianist Eugene List, comedian Jim Kirkwood, singer Dean Martin, dancer Kathryn Lee, composers Richard Rodgers and Oscar Hammerstein II, comic Jerry Lewis, fight referee Ruby Goldstein, and comedian Lee Goodman have in common?

5. Acting as spokeswoman for commercial products on the program was Julia _____.

6. What long-time member of the Sullivan entourage conducted the orchestra each Sunday evening?

7. Before achieving movie stardom, the comedy team of _____ and _____ made their television debut on the master showman's program.

Courtesy CBS.

Courtesy CBS.

Courtesy CBS.

8. The stone-faced emcee was a natural straight man for the comedic antics of a mechanical Italian mouse named _____.

9. A national hit on Italian television, the squeaky-voiced rodent was mysteriously manipulated by three people hiding behind a black velvet curtain. No one ever revealed the secret as to how the mouse could jump, dance, and move about without benefit of any strings or other visible devices. What is the English translation of this European mouse's name?

10. The Canadian team of _____ and _____ and opera singer Roberta Peters were semi-permanent fixtures in Ed's weekly lineup.

11. Sullivan instructed his cameramen to photograph gyrating rock 'n' roll singer _____ from the waist up to avoid outcries of public indignation.

12. The tight security for this special guest caused Ed to be frisked down and evicted from his own dressing room. What prominent lady was making her television singing debut on this most unusual evening?

13. When John's name flashed across the screen, the follow-up superimposed message to home viewers read, "Sorry girls. He's married." What musical group was Ed introducing to his television audience on that memorable Sunday evening in the mid-sixties?

14. Ed made frequent references to his beloved wife of many years. What was her name?

15. Although he couldn't dance, sing, or tell funny jokes, Ed Sullivan unfailingly brought the best of international entertainment to millions of American households for nearly two-and-a-half decades. Aside from the usual showcase of onstage talent he assembled each Sunday evening, Ed liked to acknowledge the presence of distinguished luminaries who were seated in his studio audience. What was Ed's familiar directive to the notables he recognized each week in his live audience?

"Father Knows Best"

Answers on pages 187–88

(1954–63)

1. Prior to the debut of this series, situation comedy "fathers" were depicted as being helpless, simple-minded bunglers. Unlike its predecessors, this series' father did indeed know best and was portrayed as being an insightful, understanding, and compassionate instructor and disciplinarian to his children. What was the name of this atypical parent?

2. Although a subsequent role in the ill-fated series "Window on Main Street" proved unsuccessful, he scored his second major television success as "Marcus Welby, M.D." What is the name of the actor who starred as the even-tempered father of TV's former first family?

3. Cancelled after only twenty-six episodes, this show was revived by the vociferous demands of its loyal viewers. After gaining a new lease on life,

the series enjoyed a 203-episode reign on television. What was Father's occupation in this long-running family series?

4. Sharing moments of both joy and sadness with her kindly husband, Jane Wyatt appeared as Father's adoring wife, _____.

5. Many episodes focused upon the family's eldest daughter and her trials and tribulations as a maturing high school student. What was her name?

6. By what pet name did Father call her?

7. Frequently scrapping with his older sister was the couple's rambunctious son, _____.

8. Youngest of the family's three children, _____ was unmistakably the apple of her father's eye.

9. What was the loving nickname Father frequently used when addressing her?

10. The setting for this weekly comedy series was the midwestern town of _____.

"The Flintstones"

Answers on page 188

(1960-66)

1. Suspiciously similar to Jackie Gleason's "The Honeymooners," this animated situation comedy featured the misadventures and domestic entanglements of two prehistoric families, the Flintstones and their next-door neighbors, Barney and Betty Rubble. In what Stone Age city did the families live?

2. Fred Flintstone operated a dinosaur crane at the local rock quarry. What was the name of the company he worked for?

3. What was the name of Fred's overbearing boss?

4. What did "Fat Freddy" expect to receive the moment he returned home from a hard day at the rockpile?

5. Upon hearing that "Daddy" was home, Fred's lovable pet dinosaur leaped up on his master, bowled him over, and licked his face with sheer delight. What was the name of the Flintstones' affectionate house pet?

6. Although he appeared regularly in an on-screen role in "The Jack Benny Program," this enormously talented comic is better known for his off-camera voices of such cartoon favorites as Bugs Bunny, Sylvester the Cat, and Daffy Duck. What is the name of the animators' mouthpiece who supplied the bark of the Flintstones' pet?

7. Although Freddy-boy was a Stone Age male chauvinist, he often ended up eating his gargantuan male ego at episode's end. What was the name of Fred's understanding wife?

8. What was her maiden name?

9. Yabba Dabba Doo! Fred's obsession with his favorite sport of _____ often interfered with his lame promises to take his wife out for a night on the town.

10. The Flintstones' car, the Flintmobile, was carved out of a tree trunk and propelled by _____ power.

11. A former regular on "The George Burns and Gracie Allen Show," "The Beverly Hillbillies," and "Petticoat Junction," _____ supplied the voice of Betty Rubble.

12. The Rubbles' son, Bamm Bamm, and the Flintstones' pretty red-haired daughter, _____, grew up together and later went steady on the updated Saturday morning "The Flintstones Comedy Hour."

13. What unusual trait separated little Bamm Bamm from the rest of the boys?

14. What were the unusual circumstances surrounding the Rubbles' adoption of this muscular tyke?

15. Shades of prehistoric Australia! The Rubbles' impish pet hoperoo, "_____," bounced his way into the hearts of series' viewers when introduced to the cast of Flintstone regulars.

16. Fred and Barney were members in good standing of The Loyal Brotherhood of _____.

17. What was the name of the local town news-slate that provided local townspeople with the daily news of 10,000 B.C.?

18. Who provided the voices for Fred and Barney in this animated sitcom?

19. In several episodes, Fred was visited by a friendly alien from the planet Zetox who unintentionally got him in a jam with family, friends, and even the law. What was the one-word name for his interplanetary guest?

20. What regular on "The Carol Burnett Show" supplied the voice for this space-age traveler?

And Away We Go!

Answers on page 189

Find the names of the following characters and personalities from variety programs in the maze of alphabet jibberish:

1. "People Are Funny" and "House Party" host
2. Baseball broadcaster who handled announcer's chores on "The Fred Waring Show"
3. Bearded "Sing Along" bandleader
4. Carol Burnett debuted on this comedian's program
5. "Candid Camera" 's Peeping Tom-host
6. Jackie Gleason's talkative bartender character
7. Banana-nosed comic who always bade goodbye to Mrs. Calabash
8. Ted Mack's "Amateur Hour" and "Family Hour" announcer
9 ."Broadway Open House" 's statuesque blonde
10. "Lonesome" comic with catch-phrase "Well, I'll be a dirty bird!"
11. Crooner fired by Arthur Godfrey for "lack of humility"
12. Newton the Bartender on "The Morey Amsterdam Show"
13. "Chesterfield Supper Club" crooner-host
14. His character creations include Cauliflower McPugg and Willy Lump Lump
15. "The Ho Ho Song" and a cupped hand over his ear were his trademarks
16. Garry Moore's long-time announcer
17. "Droodles" creator
18. Her plunging neckline caused a stir on early TV
19. "Laugh-In" 's poet laureate
20. Host of "TV Club" originating from the Terrace Casino of the Hotel Motel in Chicago

```
R E B R A B L A I S O A M I D
O A Y A M O A S G I B S O N E
O M M A Y E C I R P R O O S T
M E S G O B A V O A R A R C E
O W E R A U F A V R Y M E O D
C A M E Y D U N E K O B R U R
R I A N N Y N T H E C E R P O
E L J S N O T T U B E A H I A
L O O H E E S A X O N Y O N K
L Y E E L M A R E T O O L G Y
I A N K O A W U E S U B O L E
M C N E I L L A S M Y B A I N
M I A N D A Y I H E E L L E R
L O S T A S O R A L L O W D A
E V E H U S K E L T O N E E C
```

"The Fugitive"

Answers on page 190

(1963–67)

1. As he is returning home one evening, Dr. Richard Kimble's car lights focus upon a startled one-armed man who is fleeing from the direction of the physician's residence. Once inside his home, the ill-fated doctor discovers the lifeless, badly beaten body of his wife sprawled out on the floor. Lacking

Courtesy Worldvision Enterprises, Inc.

an alibi and known to have been quarreling recently with his wife, Kimble is accused, tried, and convicted of his spouse's murder. What actor starred as this tragic victim of circumstances?

2. Victim of the senseless crime was Kimble's wife, _____.

3. In what state was the murder of Dr. Kimble's wife committed?

4. While being transported to prison, a freak accident enables Kimble to escape. What catastrophe enabled the unjustly accused doctor to elude his captor?

Courtesy Worldvision Enterprises, Inc.

5. Kimble was relentlessly pursued by a stone-faced police lieutenant who was determined to bring his quarry to justice. What was the name of this uncompromising lawman?

6. Why was this police officer so fanatically committed to the single task of bringing Kimble in?

7. What was the name of the "hunter" 's wife (who must have been awfully lonesome with her husband running around all those years trying to catch Dr. Kimble!)?

8. What substance did the hunted physician use to alter his appearance?

9. Aside from glancing back over his shoulder at the sound of every siren or whistle, Kimble revealed his nervousness in another way. Do you remember how?

10. What was the name of the elusive one-armed man?

11. What was the name of the amputee-actor who infrequently appeared as Mrs. Kimble's murderer?

12. What was the name of Kimble's trusting sister who was instrumental in helping clear her brother's tarnished name?

13. In one of the truly classic moments in all of television broadcasting, Kimble's pursuer realizes at long last as he lies wounded in an empty amusement park midway that the doctor is innocent of the crime. What gesture of trust revealed to all of TV-land that the police lieutenant had finally come to his senses and concluded that the one-armed man was the real murderer of Kimble's wife?

14. Although the one-armed man eventually confides his guilt to Kimble while struggling with the doctor atop a tower in the deserted amusement park, the amputee-killer falls to his death before confessing to the police. Fortunately for Kimble, however, it is revealed that a neighborhood ex-serviceman had been a witness to the murder of the physician's wife. This decorated soldier had remained hidden, frozen with fear, while the one-armed man savagely pummeled Kimble's wife with his hammerlike fist. What veteran actor starred as the guilt-ridden war hero who finally agreed to step forward and reveal the truth about the tragic night in question?

15. Best known for his portrayal of the private detective "Cannon," heavy-set actor _____ narrated each "Fugitive" episode.

Courtesy Worldvision Enterprises, Inc.

"Fury"

Answers on pages 191–92

(1955–66)

1. "Fury . . . the story of a horse and the boy who loved him." What was the name of the stallion's young master?
2. Orphaned at an early age, Fury's homeless master was placed in the custody of local rancher _____ Newton.
3. Overshadowed by the television success of his brother, James Arness, _____ portrayed the orphan's adopted father in this popular Saturday-morning children's program.
4. Ann Robinson appeared as the steady girl friend of the boy's legal guardian. What was the name of the schoolteacher she portrayed?
5. What was the name of the prune-faced ranch hand who helped raise the parentless youngster?
6. Fury and his master grew up together on the _____ Ranch.
7. In what town was this small ranch located?
8. Rancher Chris Lambert's son, Packy, was the Newton boy's best friend. We all know who rode Fury, but do you recall the name of Packy's horse?
9. What was the name of Fury's "son"?
10. Yes, even horses have stage names. What was the name of the black stallion who portrayed Fury?

"The Gene Autry Show"

Answers on page 192

(1950–56)

1. Super-good guy Gene and his wonder horse _____ "followed the tumblin' tumbleweeds" through the Old West in furthering the cause of law and order.

2. What was the name of the character Gene portrayed in this wholesome Western series?

3. What was the name of the even-tempered cowpoke's familiar theme song?

4. Providing the comedy relief on Gene's action-packed Western series was the do-gooder's long-time sidekick, _____.

5. In Gene's backup singing group, a young aspiring cowboy star named Leonard Slye was on the brink of launching his own distinguished career as a Western headliner. Who was this budding star?

6. What was the name of Gene's ranch?

7. What was the name of Gene's perennial sponsor?

8. The staunch defender of range justice was brought to home viewers by Flying _____ Productions.

9. Gene waxed his own rendition of a popular children's Christmas record that sold millions of copies on the Columbia label. What was the name of the holiday favorite that rocketed the crooning cowpuncher to the top of the record charts?

10. The singing cowboy of motion picture and television fame is now a successful West Coast businessman and owner of the _____ major league baseball franchise.

Photo Quiz #1

Answers on page 192

Courtesy Hugh O'Brian

1. Who portrayed television's fearless Western lawman, Wyatt Earp?

2. What was the name of "The Jetsons" ' dog?

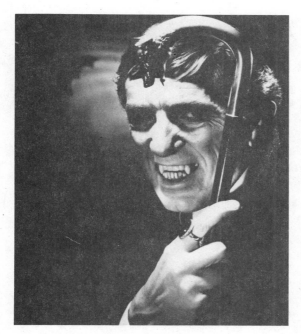

3. What was the name of the first vampire to appear in a daytime soap opera?

Courtesy National Telefilm Associates, Inc.

4. What three blonde career girls were always seeking new ways to latch onto a rich hubby in "How to Marry a Millionaire"?

Courtesy Ivan Tors Films, Inc. and Heritage Enterprises Inc.

5. What was the name of Sandy and Bud Ricks's pet dolphin?

Courtesy Worldvision Enterprises, Inc.

6. What was the name of the plainclothes detective played by Frank Converse on "N.Y.P.D."?

Courtesy Worldvision Enterprises, Inc.

7. In what town did Buffalo Bill, Jr. live with his sister, Calamity?

8. Who played George Gobel's wife, Alice, on his first television series?

Courtesy George Gobel.

9. Who was Dudley Do-Right's constant nemesis?

10. What was the name of the Deputy Chief of Operations played by Richard Webb in "U.S. Border Patrol"?

Courtesy Richard Webb Productions.

Courtesy CBS.

"Get Smart"

Answers on page 193

(1965–70)

1. "Get Smart" was a spoof of the many secret-agent series that dominated television in the mid-sixties. What actor starred as the bumbling secret agent Maxwell Smart?
2. What was the name of the secret spy agency to which Smart belonged?
3. At the beginning of each episode, Smart was seen gaining entrance to his spy agency's headquarters. How did he manage to get inside?
4. Where was the spy agency located?
5. Max's spy outfit used numbers to identify their agents. What was Smart's I.D. number?

6. Smart's female counterpart among the secret agents became his wife and mother of his twin boy and girl later in the series. Although remaining nameless on the show, she was called by her agent identification number. What was it?

7. Edward Platt starred as Maxwell Smart's beleaguered boss. By what one-word title was he always called?

8. What was his real first name?

9. What was the name of his pudgy, thickheaded assistant?

10. What code name did the spy boss use when posing as a greeting card salesman in his undercover role?

11. What sinister organization diabolically schemed each week to "get Smart"?

12. Masterminding the treacherous exploits of this clandestine spy agency was the thick-accented German agent, _____.

13. All brawn and no brain was this enemy spy agent's bulky assistant, _____.

14. Hiding in mailboxes, water fountains, clocks, and other peculiar places on undercover assignments was Secret Agent No. _____.

15. Dick Gautier played the android who occasionally teamed with Smart to thwart the forces of evil. What was the name of this mechanical secret agent?

16. Although a brilliantly written comedy series, even "Get Smart" "went to the dogs" now and then. What was the name of the undercover canine who teamed with Smart on occasion to foil the forces of international evildom?

17. Smart's apartment was well-secured and booby-trapped with a maze of door locks, guns, and even an invisible wall. What was so unusual about the klutzy secret agent's apartment number?

18. What was the name of the aged former spy agency chief who had a habit of toppling over into a comalike sleep at unexpected moments?

19. When confronted with an emergency, the nearest phone was always as close as Maxwell's _____.

20. What distinguished the pilot episode of "Get Smart" from all others that followed?

Crossword #3

Clues

Answers on page 194

Across

1. **PHOTO CLUE:** Pictured space-hero who led his Secret Squadron against the forces of evil

10. Hazel Court starred opposite him in "Dick and the Duchess"

11. Unseen puppeteer on "Kukla, Fran and Ollie"

14. "The _____ Today," pre-game football show

16. Relationship of Dr. Miguelito Lovelace to James West on "The Wild Wild West"
17. "_____, Kay," variety series hosted by Kay Westfall
18. Star of "Meet Millie" (initials)
19. Con man Sid Tomack on "My Friend Irma"
20. Film director Martin once starred in "The Paper Box," an episode of the series "Danger"
23. "_____ Witness," anthology series hosted and narrated by Richard Carlson
24. "_____ the Music," musical variety series hosted by Johnny Desmond and Shaye Cogan
26. "Can _____," celebrity stunt game show hosted by Robert Alda
28. City in which "Honey West" operated her private detective agency (abbreviation)
29. What Bernie left running when he stopped off work to see Bridgit on "Bridgit Loves Bernie"
30. "The _____ Flynn Theatre," an anthology series of dramatic productions
32. Snow (Spanish)
33. Edmund Lowe starred as David Chase, "_____ Page Detective"
36. "Baretta" 's landlord and a veteran of early live television plays (initials)
37. "All _____ Fun," variety series hosted by Charles Applewhite and George DeWitt
39. "Lights _____," anthology mystery series hosted by Frank Gallop
40. As the world's strongest insect, he shared top billing in an animated series with Secret Squirrel
44. "26 _____," tales of the Arizona Rangers
46. He starred as San Francisco attorney "Sam Benedict" (initials)
48. Every new television series hopes to be one
49. "_____ Engagement," rebroadcasts of dramas originally seen on other series
52. Spike Jones hosted the variety series "_____ Oasis"
53. "The Face _____ Familiar," game show hosted by Jack Whitaker
55. Chief Hawkeye on "Guestward Ho"
57. _____ Barnes played Myrtle on the serial "Kitty Foyle"
59. Ventriloquist Edgar Bergen hosted "_____ You Trust Your Wife?"
60. "_____ Broadway Tonight," variety series featuring new talent hosted by Rudy Vallee
61. Anita Louise served as hostess for "_____ Time"
62. "_____ Trial," starring Joseph Cotten in courtroom dramas

Down

1. "_____ File," anthology series of newspaper stories, featuring Paul Coates as host
2. "_____ Evening with Fred Astaire" in 1958 featured the superb dancer hoofing it with Barrie Chase
3. Craig Stevens starred as shamus "_____ Gunn"
4. On "The U.S. Steel Hour" 's presentation of "Beaver Patrol," Thomas _____ was featured as one of the troop's youngsters
5. "_____ About Music," a three-week series featuring calypso, American folk, and jazz
6. Name of the family on "Please Don't Eat the Daisies"
7. What Martin Milner and George Maharis did all across "Route 66"
8. John Payne as Vint Bonner, "The Restless _____"
9. Author William Somerset Maugham hosted "_____ of Tales"
12. A considerable quantity
13. Playboy casino owner Carlos Ramirez on "The Flying Nun"
15. "_____ the Facts," courtroom game show
21. "_____ _____ Lucy," legendary TV sitcom
22. James Monk and his siamese cat, Thanatopsis, told viewers one each week
24. "_____ and Fancy," anthology series featuring supernatural tales
25. "The _____ Home Show," a musical variety series hosted by Earl Wrightson
27. "The _____ Express," anthology series
31. "Redigo" 's mainliner (initials)
33. Chill Wills starred as Colonel Casey Thompson, owner of "_____ Circus"
34. "_____ Limits," science-fiction anthology hosted by Leslie Stevens
35. **PHOTO CLUE:** Space commando's scientist-friend
38. "Three on a _____," game show hosted by Bill Cullen
41. "_____, Those Bells!," sitcom featuring the antics of the Bell Brothers, custodians of the Hollywood Prop Shop
42. Dramatic series featuring Peter Graves as head of the special I.M.F. team (initials)
43. Shirley Booth portrayed widow Grace Sherwood on "A _____ of Grace"
44. Bob Keeshan briefly appeared in the series "_____ Mayor"
45. _____ _____ Horton narrated "Fractured Fairy Tales" on "Rocky and His Friends" (initials)
47. Jack Paar hosted the game show "Bank _____ the Stars"
50. "A Time for _____," soap opera dealing with the lives of sisters Linda and Jane Driscoll
51. Robert Rockwell as insurance agent Sam Logan in "The _____ from Blackhawk"

54. **PHOTO CLUE:** _____ Ferris supplied the music for this intergalactic Saturday-morning adventure series
55. Setting for "Bourbon Street Beat" (abbreviation)
56. Subsequently or thus
57. Relationship of Helen to Ann on "That Girl"
58. "Owen Marshall: Counselor _____ Law," starring Arthur Hill
59. "How _____ You Rate?," game show hosted by Tom Reddy

"Gilligan's Island"

Answers on pages 194–95

(1964–67)

1. In this series, seven castaways were stranded on an uncharted desert island after their pleasure boat ran aground. What was the name of their shipwrecked craft?

2. From what island port did the charter boat set sail? .

3. According to the show's introductory theme song, the seafarers had originally planned to take a _____-hour cruise in the calm South Pacific waters.

4. Formerly a railroad engineer in his television role as "Casey Jones," _____ portrayed the skipper of the ill-fated vessel.

5. What was the skipper's actual name?

6. Following in the footsteps of Robinson Crusoe and the Swiss Family Robinson, the wayward passengers included a crusty millionaire and his scatterbrained wife, a resourceful professor, and a voluptuous Hollywood actress. What was the name of this sexy red-headed starlet?

7. What was the name of the shapely actress who portrayed her?

8. Rounding out the group of "civilized natives" was an unpretentious "girl-next-door." What was her name?

9. From what state did she hail?

10. Forced to endure without the social amenities to which they were accustomed, millionaire-financier _____ and his patronizing wife found island life to be a distasteful experience.

11. This man of means was portrayed by boisterous actor _____.

12. What was the name of his doting spouse?

13. The inventive professor, a specialist in dull metals, was preparing a book entitled *Rust: The Real Red Menace*. At what college did the scholarly professor teach?

14. What was the rarely-spoken name of this perpetual tinkerer?

15. Whenever a plan was hatched to attempt an escape from their island prison, bungling first mate Gilligan usually managed to fumble away the crew's chances of reaching civilization. What actor graduated from his beatnik status on the "Dobie Gillis" series to appear as this nautical buffoon?

"Gunsmoke"

Answers on pages 195–96

(1955-75)

1. What cowboy movie star introduced the first "Gunsmoke" episode to millions of home viewers?

2. Arising from relative obscurity, giant-sized _____ achieved television immortality for his portrayal of Dodge City's dedicated marshal, Matt Dillon.

3. Before he cleaned up Dodge (and at the bank, too), Mister Dillon's lone claim to fame was the title role in the horror film classic _____.

4. Who is this towering 6'6" actor's real-life celebrity brother—more commonly known to TV fans as "Mr. Phelps"?

5. Matt successfully outdrew the man in black in the classic Main Street shootout at the outset of each western drama. What was the name of the television extra who succumbed to the marshal's six-iron for the show's first eight years on the tube?

6. With the original film footage wearing out, a brand new gun battle was staged for the series' ninth year on television. Original cast member Fred McDougall was selected to portray the new weekly victim of Matt Dillon's blazing six-gun. What other weekly part did McDougall play in this adult-Western saga?

73

Courtesy CBS.

7. What was the name of Marshal Dillon's horse?

8. Always concerned about Matt's safety, Amanda Blake starred as Miss Kitty, the proprietress of the _____ Saloon.

9. What was the name of the saloon's mustachioed bartender?

10. After hobbling around for many years as "Mester Dellon" 's gimpy-legged deputy-sidekick, Chester Goode, _____ became a television mainstay, appearing as a regular performer in such series as "Kentucky Jones," "Gentle Ben," and "McCloud."

11. Former skydiving co-star of "Ripcord," _____ replaced Chester as the town's cockeyed deputy, Festus Haggen.

12. What was the name of Festus's ornery mule?

13. Treating everything from headaches to bullet wounds, Milburn Stone was featured in a continuing role as the town's resident physician, Doc _____.

14. While actor Milburn Stone was recuperating from heart surgery, veteran performer _____ arrived in Dodge as the town's visiting physician to spell the venerable "Doc" during his recovery period.

15. What was the name of this stand-in physician?

16. What macho motion picture box-office headliner of the 70's once portrayed a half-breed blacksmith in this Westerner before hitting the Hollywood big time?

17. He was once described by the now-celebrated actor who portrayed him as "a guy who loves physical combat, has no prejudices, is completely independent, takes people at face value, and would just as soon fight as eat." What was the name of this half-Comanche smithy?

18. What was the name of the town's gunsmith?

19. Who was the owner of the Dodge City Boarding House?

20. In the series' seventh season, a significant change in format occurred. Do you remember what happened?

"Have Gun, Will Travel"

Answers on page 196

(1957–63)

1. What was the name of the series' gunfighter-protagonist who came to the aid of people in trouble?

2. Craggy-faced actor _____ starred as the cultured gun-for-hire who frequently quoted the literary works of Keats and Shelley.

3. What chess piece did this gunslinger adopt as his trademark?

4. The former U.S. Army officer kept a small derringer hidden in his _____ for use in times of emergency.

5. The suave gunfighter was frequently seen receiving messages from a pigtailed Chinese errand boy in the lobby of the _____ Hotel.

6. What was the name of this Oriental hotel messenger?

7. Who occasionally substituted for this Chinese run-boy to hand-carry telegrams and notes to the aristocratic gunslinger?

8. In what city did this hired gun live?

9. What was printed on the black-outfitted gunfighter's "business card"?

10. Who sang the theme song for this atypical Western drama?

Calling All Cars!

Answers on pages 196–97

Find the names of the following characters and personalities from crime dramas in the maze of alphabet jibberish:

1. "M-Squad" 's tough police lieutenant—Frank Ballinger
2. "Peter Gunn" 's nightclub hangout
3. Senior partner of "Adam-12" 's patrol team
4. "Mannix" 's original computer-run detective agency
5. Paul Burke and Horace McMahon's beat
6. "Mr. District Attorney"
7. "The Green Hornet" 's karate-chopping houseboy
8. "Paris Precinct" 's debonair gendarme
9. "Racquet Squad" 's Captain John Bradley
10. Criminologist Carl Hyatt of the "Checkmate" private detective agency
11. "The Thin Man" 's pet terrier
12. "Surfside Six" gumshoes' galpal
13. "Untouchable" racket-busting G-man—Eliot Ness
14. Shamus portrayed by William Gargan, Lee Tracy, Lloyd Nolan, and Mark Stevens
15. "Highway Patrol" Chief Dan "ten-four" Matthews
16. Original head of the Impossible Missions Force
17. Undercover policewoman "Decoy"
18. Family name of "The Defenders" father-son law practice
19. Millionaire police captain of the Metropolitan Homicide Squad
20. Captain Matt Holbrook of "The Detectives"

76

```
B A S O M E A D O T H R O M S
O T A K O A N A D R U O J E L
B A S I T L L I R A B A I Z E
L I G R H O I L O H A D L E Y
A D R A E S N O O L U I S B E
N R O B R I G G S Y A R T U V
Y O S E S L A T T A Y L O R D
A F T E O N A I T R O O W K E
S W A S P I C N O E X A R E M
H A W T E D H E D E R Y U A Y
A R E Y E R A M O G A R R L S
U C S K L A P P A G S V A O T
N O A Y A S O A H A I L B G A
I N T E R T E C T N T O B A C
E N T E S A L T E D E R Y E K
```

"Hawaiian Eye"

Answers on page 197

(1959–63)

1. This series featured the dramatic and often amorous exploits of a Hawaii-based private detective firm. What were the names of the three "Hawaiian Eyes" who formed this investigative agency?

2. The detective agency's business offices were located amidst the posh tropical surroundings of the _____ Hotel.

3. Always preoccupied with a new kooky hat, singer-photographer _____ tagged along with the shamuses on their mysterious cases.

4. What real-life singer appeared in the role of the gumshoes' galpal?

5. What was the name of the band that provided the songstress's musical accompaniment?

6. What was the name of the ukulele-playing taxicab driver who sometimes joined the detectives on one of their capers?

7. What was the name of the hotel's social director?

8. What handsome, blonde-haired actor pulled up anchor at his Miami Beach houseboat after "Surfside Six" was cancelled and joined the "Hawaiian Eye" cast as the social director of the hotel?

9. Ex-"Gilligan's Island" co-star Dawn Wells portrayed the social director's secretary in the series. What was her name?

10. Who were the two members of "Hawaii's Finest" always on the scene to make the necessary arrests at episode's end?

"Hazel"

Answers on page 198

(1961–66)

1. Created by cartoonist Ted Key for *The Saturday Evening Post*, Hazel was brought to life on television by Oscar-winning actress _____.

2. What was the irrepressible maid's last name?

3. Hazel worked as a maid for the Baxter family. The man of the house was an overweight attorney who was constantly being lectured by Hazel about his overconsumption of fattening desserts. Formerly a next-door neighbor of Ozzie and Harriet Nelson, _____ appeared as the often harassed George Baxter.

4. What was the name of Mr. Baxter's law partner?

5. What was the name of Mr. Baxter's legal secretary?

6. The counselor's attractive wife, _____, had been reared by Hazel in her formative years.

7. Mrs. Baxter turned her creative talents into a small but rewarding business. In what field of endeavor did she excel?

8. What was the name of the Baxter's son?

9. More a full-fledged member of the family than a mere domestic servant, Hazel adopted pet names for each member of the Baxter household. What were the nicknames Hazel used when addressing Mr. and Mrs. Baxter and their son?

10. What was the name of the Baxters' large shaggy dog?

11. What was the address of the Baxter family's residence?

12. What was the name of the elderly couple who lived next door to the Baxters?

13. George Baxter's most influential client was the cantankerous and bossy Mr. _____.

14. When pleased about a big deal that had just been consummated, the hard-boiled financial tycoon asked Mr. Baxter to call him by his first name— _____.

15. Hazel's delicious meals and common-sense lectures brought the tight-fisted industrialist to his knees. During these mellow moments, he often praised Hazel as being a fine woman who reminded him of someone. Who was it?

16. Hazel's regular date was the owner/dispatcher of a local taxicab company. What was the name of her harmonica-playing beau?

17. What was the name of his cab company?

18. Hazel's best friend was also her rival for the attentions of every new middle-aged Romeo who breezed into town. What was the name of the maid who formed the third party in these romantic triangles?

19. What was the name of the doctor for whom this domestic worked?

20. Hazel and her fellow maids formed a neighborhood civic organization known as the _____ Girls.

21. Hazel's talents were by no means restricted to the kitchen. Successful at almost everything she attempted, the sports-minded maid was a skillful _____, often putting on exhibitions for her local fans.

22. A frequent visitor to the Baxter kitchen while making his morning deliveries was Hazel's genial mailman-friend, _____.

23. George Baxter's socially conscious sister, _____ Thompson, was easily aggravated by Hazel's brazen attitude and seeming insolence.

24. What was the name of the wealthy Bostonite's obliging and condescending husband?

25. George's sister grabbed for the bottle of tranquilizers each time her daughter, Nancy, went out on a date with Hazel's nephew, _____.

26. The Thompsons' maid, _____, often sought professional advice from Hazel on the fine points of domestic servantry.

27. After Mr. and Mrs. Baxter left for a business trip overseas, Hazel went to work for George's brother, Steve, and his wife. Where were the original Baxters headed?

28. What was the name of Steve's wife?

29. A former Miss Arizona and 4th runner-up in the Miss America beauty pageant, _____ starred as Hazel's new mistress.

30. What was the name of the real estate salesman's daughter?

"Hogan's Heroes"

Answers on page 199

(1965–71)

1. At what German prisoner-of-war camp were Colonel Hogan and his Allied compatriots incarcerated?

2. What was Colonel Hogan's first name?

3. In what branch of the Armed Forces did Hogan serve?

4. What was Hogan's code name?

5. What was the name of the naive commandant of the military prison?

6. What was the commandant's occupation before he entered the service?

7. Who was the camp commandant's dimwitted assistant?

8. What type of company did this overweight adjutant own in his civilian life?

9. What was the name of the bald-headed commandant's curvaceous secretary?

10. Hogan and his men used their prisoner-of-war camp as a base of operation for both stealing top-secret intelligence data from their Nazi captors and assisting Allied war fugitives in making their way safely to freedom. How many "official" escapes were recorded at the prison?

11. A regular panelist on "The Match Game" and host of "Family Feud," ———— created the role of Newkirk, an English corporal in Hogan's band of "heroes."

12. What was the diminutive French Corporal Le Beau's first name?

13. What job did he perform in Hogan's undercover operation?

14. Which member of Hogan's troupe was a demolitions expert?

15. Which Hogan's "hero" operated the short-wave radio?

16. Hogan and his "heroes" traveled around the camp and outside the prison's walls through an underground network of tunnels. How did they open the secret trap door in their barracks leading down into the tunnels?

17. Where was the other entrance to the underground tunnels located?

18. What object served as the outside exit from the tunnels?

19. Hogan "bugged" conversations in the commandant's office. Where was the hidden microphone planted?

20. What appliance served as the receiver for listening in on these "bugged" conversations?

"The Honeymooners"

Answers on pages 199–200

(1955–56)

1. Jackie Gleason introduced the Honeymooner sketches to TV audiences on the "Cavalcade of Stars" in 1951. Who starred as Jackie's wife in the original version of this classic series?

2. The rotund Gleason was the architect of many hair-brained, get-rich-quick schemes in his role as bus driver Ralph ————.

3. Ralph lived in a Bensonhurst apartment building in the heart of Brooklyn. How many rooms were there in his modestly furnished apartment?

4. What was the address of Ralph's apartment building?

5. What was the name of his landlord?

6. Tenement life offered few pleasures for Ralph's downtrodden wife, ————.

7. What was his wife's maiden name?

8. What was the name of the actress who portrayed Jackie's spouse?

9. Ralph's boss at the Gotham Bus Depot was Mr. _____.

10. What was the name of the bus company's president?

11. What was the business address of the New York City bus company for whom "The Great One" worked?

12. Ralph's best friend was his sappy-looking upstairs neighbor, Ed _____.

13. What Academy Award-winning actor starred as Ralph's dimwitted pal?

14. Joyce Randolph appeared as _____, the whining wife of Ralph's empty-headed buddy.

15. During the course of a day's work, Ralph often drove over the entrance to Ed's place of business. Exactly where did the T-shirted simpleton ply his trade?

16. Each week, Ralph and his moronic pal donned their furry headgear to attend a meeting of the _____ Lodge.

17. Who was the "Grand High Exalted Ruler" of their fraternal order?

18. When "The Great One" was peeved at his wife, he swore that, "One of these days . . . Pow! _____!"

19. Angrily clenching his fist, Ralph often threatened to blast his spouse to a faraway destination. Where did he warn he would send her?

20. Many episodes ended with an apologetic Ralph embracing his all-forgiving wife and proclaiming, "Baby, _____!"

Crossword #4

Photo Courtesy National Telefilm Associates, Inc.

Answers on page 200

Clues

Across

1. **PHOTO CLUE:** He starred as a state legislator in "Slattery's People"
12. "_____ Your Way," game show hosted by Bud Collyer, John Reed King, and Kathy Godfrey
13. _____ Molinaro, Murray the cop on "The Odd Couple"
14. Ella _____ starred as "Janet Dean, Registered Nurse"
15. "The _____'s Man," starring John Compton as private detective Shannon
16. "American _____," popular weekday youth music and dance series

19. _____ Gershwin, George's lyricist brother
20. "_____ Crackerby!," starring Burl Ives as the world's richest man
21. "Twelve O'Clock _____," Air Force dramatic series starring Robert Lansing
23. What Chester A. Riley took a lot of in his hammock
25. *P.O.W.*, the first play aired on "The U.S. Steel Hour," starred Gary _____.
26. His first television series was "Talent Scouts," a variety series showcasing new talent (initials)
27. "_____, Yes Nanette," sitcom starring Miss Fabray
28. Comic who made his TV debut on the variety series "Those Two," in 1951
30. Blonde Sandy Winfield on "Surfside Six" (initials)
32. "Open _____," discussion series hosted by David Susskind
33. **PHOTO CLUE:** His secretary on "Slattery's People" was _____ Andrews
35. "The _____ Adventures of Huckleberry Finn" starred Michael Shea in the title role
37. J. Carrol Naish starred in "The _____ Adventures of Charlie Chan"
39. _____ Curtis, "Ripcord" 's skydiving Jim Buckley
42. Type of degree students were trying to achieve on "The Halls of Ivy" (abbreviation)
43. Seven-year-old _____ Rudie portrayed *Eloise* in this "Playhouse 90" comedy
46. His brother, Peter Graves, was the head of the "Mission: Impossible" force
50. "The Trials of _____" featured Peter Falk as a disheveled attorney
52. The city that provided the setting for "Alarm" (abbreviation)
55. Philip _____ played Jake Goldberg in "The Goldbergs"
56. Paul Burke and Vic Rodman were veterinarians on "_____ Ark"
58. _____ Edwards, distinguished CBS newscaster
61. One of the leads on "The Henny and Rocky Show" (initials)
62. "The U.S. Steel Hour" 's production of *Incident in _____ Alley* starred Farley Granger as a guilt-ridden cop who had killed a youth fleeing the scene of a crime
63. Dick Button starred in _____ *Brinker or The Silver Skates*, a 1958 "Hallmark Hall of Fame" production
64. The dramatic tales of Jane and Linda Driscoll were featured in "A Time For _____"
65. "_____ Pun", game show hosted by Johnny Bradford

Down

1. Richard Greene played this legendary outlaw who robbed from the rich and gave to the poor

84

2. "The _____ _____ Hutton Show," musical variety series
3. Owned or possessed
4. Belonging to one of the Ritz Brothers, hosts of "The All-Star Revue"
5. "This Is Galen _____," variety series
6. "_____ You Top This?," game show featuring Senator Edward Ford as the "Joke Teller"
7. Relieve
8. Newsman who tracked the fabled *Orient Express* train in 1964 (initials)
9. _____ Brand appeared as mobster Al "Scarface" Capone on "The Untouchables"
10. He delivered his "Football Forecasts" in the early fifties (initials)
11. "_____ _____, Will Travel," Western series
17. Fonzie kisses his girls on the _____, or back of the neck
18. _____ Poston, panelist on "To Tell the Truth" and host of the game show "Split Personality"
21. "_____ Mom," featuring Shari Lewis, Josephine McCarthy, and Jane Palmer
22. Astronaut John _____ faced pint-sized actor Eddie Hodges on the musical quiz show "Name That Tune"
24. Supersonic Transport (abbreviation)
29. Veteran TV comedienne, Barbara _____
31. _____ Kaye starred in a "See It Now" program dealing with the work of UNICEF
33. **PHOTO CLUE:** Role pictured star played on "The Real McCoys"
34. "_____ Grey Theatre," Western series hosted and narrated by Dick Powell
36. "The _____," anthology dramas about people caught in perilous dilemmas
38. "_____ of the World," serial starring Gloria Louis
40. _____ Arden, one of "The Mothers-in-Law"
41. This legendary comedian's daughter, Joan, appeared with him on a 1954 program
44. "_____ Line," game show hosted by Dick Van Dyke
45. He played "Martin Kane, Private Eye"
46. "You _____ There," hosted by Walter Cronkite
47. "Adam's _____," sitcom based on the movie of the same title
48. Section of the country where "The Funky Phantom" took place (abbreviation)
49. "Shotgun _____," starring Scott Brady in the lead role
51. "_____ Lady," starring Lynn Bari as Gwen Allen, owner-operator of the Hillendale Homes Construction Company
53. He played "Casey Jones," railroad engineer (initials)
54. "Rhoda" 's mother

57. Howard K. Smith and Eric Sevareid were also featured on the news documentary "_____ It Now"
59. "Chevrolet _____ Broadway," musical variety series hosted by Snooky Lanson
60. He played Rusty on "Rin Tin Tin" (initials)
61. Newscaster who moderated the televised Kennedy-Nixon debates in 1960 (initials)

"Hopalong Cassidy"

Answers on page 201

(1949-51)

1. Characteristically attired in his all-black cowboy outfit and sporting two pearl-handled revolvers, _____ thrilled youngsters in his role as cowboy hero Hopalong Cassidy.
2. What was Hopalong's nickname?
3. What was the name of the silver-haired hero's wonder horse?
4. What color was Hopalong's obedient stallion?
5. A former commercial spokesman for Quaker Puffed cereals, grizzled _____ appeared as one of Hopalong's many sidekicks.
6. Edgar Buchanan also teamed with Hopalong to track down bank robbers and cattle rustlers. What was the name of the paunchy cowpoke he portrayed?
7. Name two other cowpunchers who rode with Hopalong as his trusted companion.
8. With the bad guys safely behind bars in the local jail, Hopalong rode off into the sunset toward his ranch, the _____.
9. In what city was his ranch located?
10. What was the name of the author who created the now-legendary Hopalong Cassidy character shortly after the turn of the century?

Courtesy Bob Smith.

"The Howdy Doody Show"

Answers on pages 201–2

(1947–60)

1. What was the original title of this enormously popular children's series?

2. What was the name of the ex-disc jockey with the buckskin outfit who presided over the show's festivities?

3. In what state was Howdy Doody born?

4. Who supplied Howdy's voice?

5. The town of Doodyville was inhabited with many interesting marionette characters. Included among them were John J. Fedoozel—America's No. 1 (Boing!) Private Eye, Sidesaddle Sol, and the storekeeper for the mythical village. What was this puppet merchant's name?

6. What was Clarabell the Clown's last name?

7. Although he never uttered a word during the show's long run on television (except for a "Good-bye, kids" in the final program), Clarabell was able to communicate with all his friends. How did he manage this feat?

8. Currently the star of a children's television series, _____ first enacted the role of the mischievous, seltzer-spraying clown on Howdy's show.

9. What was the name of the evil clown who often harassed poor Clarabell?

10. Howdy's pet was a strange-looking composite of many different animal types. What was the name of the creature with the flowerpot hat?

11. What was the favorite dish of Howdy's animal friend?

12. Howdy's timid companion, _____, demonstrated unusual dexterity by wiggling his ears.

13. Villainous Mr. _____ was the cantankerous mayor of the marionette village.

14. What was the name of the grumpy troublemaker's nephew?

15. Featured on the show were a beautiful Indian princess and her tribal chieftain. What were the names of Howdy's Indian friends?

16. What was the Chief's familiar one-word exclamation of surprise?

17. What was the name of Howdy's twin brother?

18. What was the name of the cowboy marionette's dancing elephant pal?

19. Spinning her wondrous tales of fun and adventure was the Story Princess, _____.

20. Howdy was presented with a television female cousin when _____ Doody was introduced to the marionette cast later in the series.

21. What was the name of the seaworthy captain who piloted his ship down the calm waters of Doodyville Bay?

22. Oil Well _____ was Doodyville's friendly prospector.

23. What was the name of Doodyville's local band of musicians?

24. Singer Marti Barris arrived in Doodyville as the first human female resident since actress Judy Tyler's tragic death. What was the name of the pretty teenager with the candy-striped shirt she portrayed?

25. Wide-eyed screaming youngsters delighted to the antics of Howdy and all his friends from their seats in the "_____ Gallery."

"I Dream of Jeannie"

Answers on page 202

(1965–70)

1. After overshooting his splashdown target, astronaut _____'s spacecraft washes up on the shore of a deserted island where he finds a bottle containing the impish genie.

2. Jeannie had been "bottle-wrecked" for _____ years before being discovered by her twentieth-century master.

3. Loyal to her master's every wish, _____ starred as the scantily-clad lady of the bottle.

4. Where was Jeannie born?

5. What was the name of the genie who imprisoned Jeannie in her bottle when she refused to marry him?

6. Formerly Cochise on "Broken Arrow," _____ starred as this most powerful and feared genie.

7. Jeannie's master was engaged to his commanding officer's daughter when he first met his "lady of the bottle." What was the name of the "other woman" who was quickly to become the astronaut's ex-fiancée?

8. The master's best friend was a fellow bachelor astronaut who spent most of his leisure moments chasing girls. Bill Daily was featured each week as the carefree Major _____.

9. How did Jeannie summon her magical powers into action?

10. How many earthly mortals knew of her "genie-ological" history?

11. Where did Jeannie and her master live?

12. Trying desperately to seek rational explanations for the bizarre events created by Jeannie's magic was the frustrated base psychiatrist, Dr. _____.

13. Emmaline Henry starred as the shrink's wife, _____.

14. What was the name of the austere general who commanded the Cocoa Beach space installation where the astronauts were stationed?

15. Who was the "Master of all Genies"?

16. Former regular series performer on "Dobie Gillis", "The Good Guys", and "Gilligan's Island," Bob Denver turned up as _____, bumbling son of the "Master of all Genies."

17. What was the name of Jeannie's sister?

18. Who was her sister's master?

19. What was the name of Jeannie's dog-genie?

20. Although she appeared as the mother of Jeannie's astronaut master in this series, television viewers will best remember her as Lily Ruskin in "December Bride." What was the name of this distinguished actress?

"I Love Lucy"

Answers on page 203

(1951–57)

1. Lucille Ball starred as the zany wife of a high-strung Cuban bandleader. What was the name of the madcap housewife she portrayed in the series?

2. What was the trouble-prone redhead's maiden name?

3. Lucy's excitable Latin hubby, _____, babbled angrily in his native tongue when exasperated by his wife's antics.

4. Appearing as the conga-playing bandleader was Lucy's former real-life husband, _____.

5. At what club did the Cuban entertainer perform?

6. Pounding a large conga drum, Lucy's husband could be heard bellowing out his favorite song, "_____," during each performance at the club.

7. The birth of Lucy's TV baby was the cover story in the first issue of a now-famous weekly publication. Do you recall which one?

8. The couple's preschool son was an accomplished drummer. What was the name of their child prodigy?

9. What was the address of the apartment building where Lucy lived?

10. The couple's old and seemingly decrepit upstairs babysitter at their Manhattan apartment building was Mrs. _____.

11. The duo's inseparable companions were their downstairs landlord neighbors, _____ and _____ Mertz.

12. Potbellied funnyman William _____ and Lucy's co-star in a later series, Vivian _____, played the Mertzes.

Courtesy CBS.

13. What line of work were the Mertzes in before getting into the landlord business?

14. Lucy encountered some rough sailing and a boatload of embarassing moments when she ran up against her husband's Uncle _____ while vacationing in Cuba.

15. Lucy's hubby packed up and took the whole gang with him when he went out to Hollywood to star in his first movie. What was the name of the film that brought this Latin singer to Tinsel Town?

Say, Kids! What Time Is It?

Answers on pages 203–4

Find the names of the following characters and personalities from children's programs in the maze of alphabet jibberish:

1. Ovaltine-drinking space-hero
2. "Rin Tin Tin" 's pint-sized master
3. Don Herbert's scientific title
4. "Mr. I Magination"
5. "Ding Dong School" 's finger-painting teacher
6. "Underdog" 's off-screen voice
7. Feline Ruff's doggy companion
8. "Super Circus" 's ravishing blonde bandleader
9. Quick Draw McGraw's Mexican sidekick
10. "Annie Oakley" 's kid brother
11. Kukla and Ollie's female co-star
12. Cliff Robertson's "Rocket Ranger" role
13. Ventriloquist-creator of puppets Lamb Chop and Hush Puppy
14. Bullwinkle Moose's flying squirrel pal
15. Rootie Kazootie's arch-nemesis
16. Choo Choo, Benny the Ball, and The Brain's alley cat chieftan
17. Winky Dink's canine friend
18. Beanie's seasick sea serpent
19. *The Songbird*'s flying cowboy-pilot
20. Crabby Appleton's innocent prey

```
B R A S H O S P R O N A I G H
L O C H A U P L E W I S N Y E
I C T E M M O O G A N I T O C
S K O A M E R V U S K R E A E
A Y C Y C E C I L Y O U P Y D
G E X O A P O N K I R T E E R
O O S D T O O S O L M E B R A
C O Y E R S Y T A I D R U E Z
U L O L I H E A D R U R N D I
P A I L P O G N E R L I P O W
A B L E P L I G E A L F A R R
S A Y R O G E F Y T O I C U M
E B A I H O O F R A N C E S E
K O U T E O J A I G A H A T H
O B R O W N H E N G R E L Y E
```

"The Jack Benny Show"

Answers on page 204

(1950–65)

1. In this vintage situation comedy, Jack portrayed the star of a weekly television series. Do you remember the name of his gravel-voiced valet?

2. Famous for supplying cartoon voices, _____ appeared in the series as Jack's agonizing French violin teacher, Professor LeBlanc.

3. Too cheap to purchase a new automobile, skinflint Jack owned a touring car of a bygone era. What type of car did Benny drive?

4. Jack's real-life wife and wisecracking onstage girl friend, Mary Livingstone, worked at the May Company Department Store. Who played the mustachioed floorwalker who responded to his page with an elongated "Y-y-y-e-s-s?"?

5. Benny acted the part of such a notorious, penny-pinching tightwad that he was once accused of "assault-and-battery" upon President Lincoln! Where did the miserly comedian keep his coveted wealth stored?

6. Jack's frequent run-ins with the Beverly Hills police provided some of the show's never-to-be-forgotten moments. What was so unusual about the local police station's telephone number?

7. What movie starlet made her television debut on Jack's show in 1953?

8. What was the name of the singing quartet with the vocalized hum that delivered their musical sales pitch to Jack's viewers?

9. Veteran actress Bea Benaderet showed up in the series as Jack's switchboard operator, _____.

10. Who taught Jack's parrot how to talk?

11. What famous funnyman supplied the voice of the miser's unusual pet bird?

12. Jack pranced onstage each week to the strains of his familiar theme song, "_____."

13. At the conclusion of each week's sketch, the show's jovial, heavy-set announcer, _____, informed the television audience, "Jack will be back in a moment."

14. The effeminate-acting comedian always fibbed about his true age, maintaining that he was only _____ years old year after year.

15. What was the name of the "Waukegan Penny Pincher"'s dessert sponsor?

Courtesy Wrather Corporation.

"Lassie"

Answers on pages 204–6

(1954–72)

1. Lassie had several television families during her long tenure on the small screen. What was the name of the bright-eyed youngster who appeared as the collie's first master, Jeff Miller?

2. Jeff lived in the country with his widowed mother, _____, and his beloved "Gramps."

3. The Millers lived on a small farm on the outskirts of the city of _____.

4. How did Jeff acquire Lassie?

5. Jeff's familiar cry of "Ee-ya-kee!" signaled his best friend that he was rapidly approaching on his bicycle. Always wearing a crown-shaped cap, Porky _____ was Jeff's inseparable companion.

6. What was Porky's actual first name?

Courtesy Wrather Corporation.

7. Jeff's portly friend owned a slow-footed dachshund who often hitched rides in the basket of his bicycle. What was the appropriate name of this lazy pet?

8. Jeff's chubby companion lived on a neighboring farm with his checker-playing father, _____.

9. When Lassie was sick or injured, the Millers quickly summoned the local veterinarian for help. What was this country doctor's name?

10. What was the name of Jeff's colt?

11. The Millers had a hand-cranked telephone on their kitchen wall. What was the name of the friendly operator who assisted them in placing their calls?

12. What was the name of the Millers' family physician?

13. When actor George "Gramps" Cleveland died during the filming of the series, the cast of the perennial Sunday-night favorite was revised. Unable to properly care for the farm alone, Jeff's mother sold the property to _____ and _____ Martin.

14. An Academy Award-winner and situation comedy veteran, _____ played Mrs. Martin on the show.

15. The Martins' adopted seven-year-old son, _____, became Lassie's second television master.

16. In still a third change in casting, June Lockhart and Hugh Reilly became parents of the small boy and owners of the farmhouse. What was the name of the kindly uncle who tenanted the farmhouse with them?

17. In yet another housecleaning move by the show's producers, the Martins left their idyllic country surroundings to assist homesteaders till their farmland in the Australian bush country. Because of strict quarantine laws, the Martins were forced to leave Lassie behind. Who was Lassie left with?

18. Soon thereafter, Lassie's new master suffered a heart attack and was forced to give up his magnificent collie. Lassie was given to a leather-faced forest ranger who had rescued the collie and nursed her back to health in a special five-part episode earlier in the series. What was the name of the ranger who became Lassie's new master?

19. Lassie's trainer, _____, cast male dogs in the title role because they were easier to handle.

20. Who was the long-time sponsor of this perennial children's favorite?

"Leave It to Beaver"

Answers on page 206

(1957–63)

1. Who starred as the mischievous title character, Beaver Cleaver?

2. Beaver was rarely called by his real name. Do you remember what it was?

3. Hugh Beaumont and Barbara Billingsley portrayed the Beaver's no-nonsense parents. What were the first names of his firm but understanding mother and father?

Courtesy CBS.

4. When Beaver was being reprimanded by his father, his older brother, Wally, tried to hang around to watch the fireworks. Who appeared as Beaver's big brother?

5. In what city did Beaver and his family reside?

6. The Beaver's closest friend was usually seen munching on something to eat. What was the name of his stout chum?

7. Beaver was often taunted by an overgrown, pigtailed girl who sat in the "smart row" at the neighborhood school. What was the name of this snotty tease?

8. Reading, writing, and arithmetic did not come easily to the Beaver. On several occasions, notes were sent home to Beaver's parents from his pretty young teacher, Miss _____.

9. As with any other red-blooded American schoolboy, Beaver preferred recess to his other subjects, fidgeted in his seat during the long school day, and disliked having to do his homework. Do you remember the name of the fun-loving tyke's school principal?

10. What was the last name of the Beaver's schoolmate and close friend, Whitey?

11. Beaver occasionally stopped by the fire station on his way home from school to chat with the elder member of the hook-and-ladder squad. What was the name of this old-time firefighter?

12. Wally's sickeningly sweet friend, _____, patronized Mrs. Cleaver with his insincere compliments.

13. Bullying smaller playmates was a favorite pastime of Wally's oafish friend, Clarence Rutherford. By what nickname was this jelly-belly more commonly known?

14. Clarence tucked his tail between his legs and went whimpering home to his "Daddy" whenever Wally or one of his pals stood his ground and refused to back down. What veteran television star appeared as the bully's over-protective father?

15. Clarence's father, _____, made his son march straight over to the Cleaver household and apologize whenever his boy was clearly responsible for instigating a neighborhood altercation.

And Here's Your Host...

Answers on page 207

Find the names of the hosts of the following game shows in the maze of alphabet jibberish:

1. "Pantomime Quiz"
2. "Queen for a Day"
3. "Dotto"
4. "Play Your Hunch"
5. "The $64,000 Challenge"
6. "Beat the Clock"
7. "Two for the Money"
8. "The Price Is Right"
9. "Do You Trust Your Wife?"
10. "Treasure Hunt"
11. "The Who, What or Where Game"
12. "I've Got a Secret"
13. "Do Re Mi"
14. "Stop the Music"
15. "It Could Be You"
16. "Masquerade Party"
17. "What's My Line?"
18. "Strike It Rich"
19. "Name That Tune"
20. "Twenty-One"

```
Z O Y E A H O S K A L O D E B
A R E S C U L L E N O D O L A
I C K A S L U I T E E Y R A R
M O O L E L D R O W R D O I R
A I T L E Y O R I R E A Y S Y
U K S A L E A T H I S L O E E
S O A N E Y T A I C A Y L A L
B T R O B I E T Z O S A D O I
Y E O U Y S K R A P O L E N A
A T R R O Y A S E R A I W O B
I N O G Y N I K Y N D R O J E
M O O R E E S O O L I A P A D
U B R O A N O D Y A Z R O M Y
L Y A R R U M O A X E C H E N
D E M E G R I F F I N E A S E
```

"The Life of Riley"

Answers on pages 207–8

(1953–58)

1. The prototype of the bungling husband in television situation comedy, veteran actor _____ starred as that lovable oaf, Chester A. Riley.
2. Riley lived in a small white cottage at 1313 _____ Terrace.

3. During the introduction to each episode, a caricature of Riley was seen lounging comfortably in a _____.

4. Riley worked as a hard-hatted construction worker at the _____ Aircraft Company.

5. What type of work did Riley do at the plant?

6. Riley was frequently at odds with his plant foreman. What was his name?

7. One of Riley's fellow workers at the plant was a bulky, good-natured simpleton who always wore a tam-o'-shanter. What was his name?

8. Marjorie Reynolds lent a note of credibility as Riley's sensible wife, _____.

9. What were the names of Riley's two children?

10. The Rileys' closest friends were their upstairs duplex neighbors, _____ and _____ Gillis.

11. What was Mrs. Gillis's pet name for her hubby?

12. What was the name of the Gillises' young son?

13. In what city did the Rileys live?

14. A transplanted New Yorker, Riley remained faithful to his native Flatbush by joining the _____ after settling into his new sun-drenched surroundings.

15. After coming into a large sum of money, the Gillises moved out of the neighborhood and entrusted Riley with the rental of their little white cottage. What was the name of the shiftless loafer and his plump blonde wife who leased the Gillises' home from Riley?

16. Riley's daughter finally tied the knot with her ex-Marine boyfriend before the series left the air. Later the co-star of a weekly police series, boyish-looking _____ appeared as her serviceman beau, Don Marshall.

17. The couple quickly presented Riley with a grandson—Baby _____.

18. Usually found tinkering around in his garage, Sterling Holloway appeared as Riley's ingenious professor-friend, _____.

19. Exasperated by the predicament he usually found himself in at the conclusion of each episode, Riley would face the camera and bemoan, "_____."

20. Surprisingly, the first "Life of Riley" television series debuted in 1949. Who starred as Mr. and Mrs. Riley in this vintage predecessor to the more widely remembered mid-fifties version of the comedy series?

Courtesy Wrather Corporation.

"The Lone Ranger"

Answers on page 208

(1949–61)

1. What was the name of the Texas Ranger who adopted the guise of "The Lone Ranger"?
2. Who was the first actor to portray the masked man?
3. Who took over the role in the series' second year and achieved television immortality with his portrayal?
4. The "mysterious stranger" rode a beautiful white stallion named _____.

5. Jay Silverheels played the Lone Ranger's "faithful Indian companion," _____.

6. To what tribe did the masked man's sidekick belong?

7. What was the name of his Indian companion's brown-and-white pinto?

8. The Lone Ranger was known to his Indian comrade as "_____," a name meaning "faithful friend."

9. The Lone Ranger fired bullets made of _____, a telltale trademark of the masked rider.

10. At the conclusion of each episode, the Lone Ranger's horse reared up on its hindlegs as the Ranger cried out commandingly, "_____."

"Love That Bob"

Answers on pages 208–9

(1954–61)

1. Handsome Bob Cummings starred as _____, a womanizing commercial photographer who specialized in shapely models.

2. Bob lived with his widowed sister and girl-crazy nephew. What were their names?

3. What was the name of the airline pilot who courted Bob's sister?

4. Whom did Bob's nephew date on a steady basis?

5. What was the name of Bob's girl Friday?

6. What was the name of her sailor beau?

7. Bob had all he could handle when visited by his fun-loving grandpa. What was the name of this peppery old rascal?

8. From what midwestern city did Bob's grandpa hail?

9. What actor created the role of Bob's spry grandpa?

10. What was the name of Grandpa Collins's antique car?

11. What was Grandpa's former profession?

12. Buxom Joi Lansing appeared in the series as _____, a sexy blonde model who was always trying to latch onto Bob.

13. What was the name of Bob's henpecked Army buddy who catered to his wife Ruthie's every wish?

14. Although constantly surrounded by curvaceous models, Bob held a special place in his heart for his true love, _____.

15. Nancy Culp made frequent appearances as Bob's birdwatcher-friend. What was her name?

"Make Room for Daddy"

Answers on pages 209–10

(1953–64)

1. Paralleling his own career as a nightclub entertainer, Danny Thomas appeared relaxed and natural in his portrayal of singer-comedian Danny _____.

2. In the early version of the series, Danny and his wife, Margaret, lived with their two adorable children in a New York City apartment. What were the names of their lovable tykes?

3. What was Danny's New York address?

4. What was the name of the family's pet terrier?

5. Danny became a widower in the series when his first television wife, actress _____, departed the cast in 1957.

6. Forced to assume the role of both father and mother to his children, Danny found himself in a quandary until he met his future bride-to-be. What was the name of the woman who rescued Danny from the loneliness and despair of widowerhood?

7. What was the maiden name of Danny's second TV wife?

8. What was her occupation at the time she met Danny?

9. Danny gained another child through his remarriage on the show. Angela Cartwright was introduced to the cast as the club entertainer's stepdaughter, _____.

10. What was the name of Danny's kindly father-confessor press agent and close friend in the series?

11. What was the name of Danny's piano accompanist?

Courtesy Maury Foldare & Associates.

12. Arriving at unexpected moments to check up on his favorite nephew and his family was Danny's boisterous Uncle _____.

13. Originally cast in the series as the cousin of Danny's first wife, "Pantomine Quiz" regular _____ schooled the family in Lebanese custom and tradition as the take-charge uncle.

14. Danny's transplanted Lebanese uncle resided in the midwestern city of _____.

15. What was the name of the family's housekeeper?

16. At what club did Danny appear as a regular performer?

17. Once the trusty sidekick to television's Captain Midnight, diminutive comic _____ starred as the club's hyperactive owner, Charley Halper.

18. Comedienne Pat Carroll made infrequent appearances as the wife of Danny's excitable boss. What was Mrs. Halper's animal-sounding first name?

19. What was the name of Danny's apartment house landlord?

20. A veteran of television situation comedy, having appeared in such series as "The Brothers," "Our Miss Brooks," and "The Lucy Show," _____ infrequently appeared as the complaining landlord.

21. What was the name of the janitor of the apartment building?

22. After making his television debut on "The Steve Allen Show," _____ re-created his popular character José Jiminez, Latin antagonist to the English language, in this series.

23. What part did he play in the show?

24. What was the name of Danny's songwriter?

25. Ex-movie heavy _____ was injected into the cast as yet another of Danny's agents, Phil Brokaw.

26. What was the name of the Italian foreign exchange student who came to live with Danny and his family when their eldest daughter went away to college?

27. What former "Mickey Mouse Club" Mouseketeer appeared in this role?

28. After Danny's eldest daughter returned from college overseas, she fell in love with and, in a whirlwind courtship, married a young comedian who was appearing on the same nightclub bill as Danny. What was the name of her spouse?

29. Originally picked to fill Danny's shoes after he retired from the series, ex-Jack Paar regular _____ was bumped from the cast at season's end after his marriage to the nightclub entertainer's daughter.

30. What characterization did this quickly deposed comedian create on Paar's nighttime show?

Photo © 1978 P.A.T.—Ward.

Answers on page 210

Clues

Across

1. **PHOTO CLUE:** The flying squirrel star who appeared in a series with his "Friends"

4. "_____ _____," starring Patrick McGoohan as NATO investigator John Drake

10. Players picked questions from "The Dunce Cap" on "It Pays to _____ Ignorant"

11. Gene Barry appeared as Western law enforcer whose first and middle names were William Bartley
12. "Double _____ Nothing," early game show hosted by Bert Parks
13. "The _____," starring Robert Conrad as Paul Ryan
14. As Bruce Crawford, he was engaged to Ann Flood on the serial "From These Roots" (initials)
16. Description of Dick Van Dyke's physique
18. _____ Davis, singer-composer who has been a series headliner
20. "_____ America," early morning news program
21. PHOTO CLUE: The squirrel star's thick-headed moose friend
23. "That Reminds _____," game show hosted by Arlene Francis
24. Admiral Harriman Nelson on "Voyage to the Bottom of the Sea" (initials)
25. City that formed setting for "The Roaring Twenties" (abbreviation)
26. Alan _____, Pasquale on "Life with Luigi"
30. "The _____ Game," movie quiz show hosted by Jack Barry
32. "_____ Court," featuring Jay Jostyn as the judge
35. Jack Lord starred as rodeo champion "Stoney _____"
38. Soap opera, "_____ the World Turns"
39. "Quick _____a Flash," game show hosted by Bobby Sherwood
40. "The _____ Carroll Show," comedy series
41. "_____ Magic," hosted by Paul Tripp
43. "_____ at Eleven," variety series hosted by George DeWitt
47. _____Dawson, handyman on "Green Acres"
49. Occupation of Hal March in "The Soldiers" (abbreviation)
50. What "Mr. Novak" did
52. He drove campers crazy by stealing their picnic baskets at Jellystone National Park
54. "_____ Million," a segment of "NBC Mystery Movie"
56. Pinky Lee always wore a checkered one
58. "Sha Na _____," musical group with their own syndicated series
61. "The New _____ Revue," children's program featuring Doug, Emmy Joe, Charlie the owl, Freddie the frog, Henrietta the hippo, and Mr. Dingle, the storekeeper
62. "_____-Honestly," comedy series set in London

63. "The Young and the _____," soap opera situated in Genoa City
64. What "The Magic Clown," Zorella, often performed

Down

1. His intergalactic "Rocket Rangers" operated from their Omega Base
2. What Claude Akins and Frank Converse used to talk with other truckers on "Movin' On"
3. "Bachelor Father" 's niece

4. "The _____ Kaye Show," featuring Harvey Korman, Vikki Carr, and Joyce Van Patten
5. "Garroway _____ Large" was Dave's first TV series
6. His girl friend was Lou Ann Poovie
7. A period of time
8. "Pinky" 's first name in "Adam's Rib"
9. "_____ That Tune," musical game show
11. Barbara _____ appeared with her real-life husband, Martin Landau, on "Mission: Impossible"
15. What the *Seaview* was on "Voyage to the Bottom of the Sea"
17. Comedian nicknamed "The Perfect Fool" appeared on television in a situation comedy, variety series, and in dramatic productions (initials)
19. Sonny' former on-and-off set partner
22. Regular panelist on "To Tell the Truth" and "What's Going On?" (initials)
27. "_____ Phoebe," starring Peter Lawford as lovelorn columnist Bill Hastings
28. **PHOTO CLUE:** Mr. _____ used his evil agents, Boris Badenov and Natasha Fataly, to combat the squirrel-hero and his faithful moose friend
29. "The Cattanooga _____," animated cartoon series
31. What two of the three contestants on "To Tell the Truth" were asked to do
33. Game show, "_____ Got a Secret"
34. "_____ Christian Anderson," anthology series based on fairy tales
35. "_____Father," starring John Forsythe as attorney Bentley Gregg
36. "Tell _____More," documentaries of famous celebrities
37. Frontier scout portrayed by Bill Williams on a Western series
40. He starred as nightclub comedian Joey Barnes ·with Abby Dalton and Corbett Monica on a situation comedy
41. Irritating sensation
42. City in which "Checkmate" took place (abbreviation)
44. _____ Marshall, Dr. Ben Craig on "The Bold Ones" ' segment, "The Doctors"
45. Messrs. Damone and Morrow
46. One of the three major commercial television networks
48. What Lassie and Rin Tin Tin loved to chew on
50. Sound made by the tugboat *Cheryl Ann* on "Waterfront"
51. "_____," situation comedy starring Dick Kallman trying to earn a degree at Western State University
53. What Gomer and Goober both pumped on "The Andy Griffith Show"
55. *The Wizard of* _____, movie rebroadcast each year starring Judy Garland
57. "Draw _____ Win," game show hosted by Henry Morgan
59. "The _____ Capp Show," discussion series
60. "Where the Action _____," rock show hosted by Dick Clark

"The Man from U.N.C.L.E."

Answers on page 211

(1964–68)

1. U.N.C.L.E. was a global law enforcement agency bent on suppressing threats to international peace. What do the letters in the acronym U.N.C.L.E. stand for?

2. Robert Vaughn appeared as the Chief Enforcement Agent for the international security organization. What was the name of the undercover operative he portrayed?

3. What was his agent identification number?

4. Teaming with Vaughn in his pursuit of international lawbreakers was his methodically efficient, Soviet-born associate. David McCallum starred as the impassive, technologically-oriented agent, _____.

5. The Chief of Section One of U.N.C.L.E. monitored the field activities of the American agent and his Russian counterpart from the agency's home office. Formerly the star of the "Topper" comedy series, bushy-browed _____ created the role of the organization's pipe-smoking watchdog, Mr. Waverly.

6. What was Mr. Waverly's first name?

7. What type of retail establishment posed as a front for U.N.C.L.E. headquarters?

8. Who owned the store containing the secret entrance to the worldwide law enforcement agency?

9. In what city was the super-spy agency located?

10. What was the name of the Chief Agent's efficient girl Friday who was occasionally featured on the program?

11. What was the name of the attractive U.N.C.L.E. researcher who worked in both the Personality Introduction and Research Information Centers?

12. When she had some spare time on her hands, this ambitious agency employee also worked in the _____ Division.

13. Communications with U.N.C.L.E. headquarters were accomplished through the use of a miniature transceiver cleverly concealed in a small object the agents carried in their breast pockets. Exactly where was the communications device hidden?

14. U.N.C.L.E. agents were constantly locked in a bitter struggle with an undercover criminal organization known as _____.

15. What was the name of the spin-off spy series that originated as a pilot on this series?

"The Many Loves of Dobie Gillis"

Answers on pages 211–12

(1959–63)

1. Who starred as Dobie "all play and no work makes me a happy boy" Gillis?

2. Dobie lived with his parents in the apartment directly above the family's store. What did his folks do for a living?

3. What was the address of the building in which the family store and home was located?

4. In what city did Dobie and his family reside?

5. What was the name of Dobie's dad?

6. Dobie's father frequently bragged about a medal he had received while serving his country. What was this cherished medal?

7. What was the name of Dobie's mother?

8. What was the name of Dobie's beatnik sidekick?

9. What was his stock response whenever someone called his name?

10. What neighborhood event was he forever asking Dobie to go watch with him?

11. What was this hipster's favorite movie?

12. What color was Dobie's hair when the series debuted?

13. What color was it later changed to?

14. Who portrayed the heartthrob of Dobie's life, blonde-haired beauty Thalia Menninger?

15. What was the name of the rich kid in town who competed with Dobie for Thalia's affections?

16. What current motion picture star appeared early in his acting career as this well-heeled society lad?

17. What was the name of the wealthy teen's mother?

18. Later in the series, a new rich and spoiled teenager was injected into the cast. What was the name of the high society youngster who called Dobie "Dobie doo"?

19. What was the name of Dobie's brother?

20. Coincidentally, what actor portrayed Dobie's sibling in the series?

21. What was the name of the not-so-glamorous girl who kept trying to snare Dobie as her boyfriend?

22. Later to appear as Patty Duke's father in another television sitcom, _____ made frequent appearances as Mr. Pomfritt, Dobie's high school English teacher.

23. What was the name of the Oriental owner of the ice cream parlor where Dobie and his friends hung out after school?

24. In a change in the show's format, Dobie and his beatnik "good buddy" enlisted in the Army. What was the name of the boys' commanding officer?

25. Who created this teen-oriented situation comedy?

Photo Quiz #2

Answers on page 212

1. How much did "Gentle Ben" weigh?

Courtesy Ivan Tors Films, Inc. and Heritage Enterprises Inc.   113

Courtesy Ralph Edwards Productions.

2. Who hosted the sentimental, nostalgic tributes on "This Is Your Life"?

© *1978 Hanna-Barbera Productions, Inc.*

3. How many of these Hanna-Barbera animated television characters can you identify?

Courtesy Telewide Systems, Inc.

4. Who portrayed the Cisco Kid (right) and his inseparable companion, Pancho?

5. Who acted as "our guide into the world of the unknown" in "One Step Beyond"?

Courtesy Worldvision Enterprises, Inc.

Courtesy Worldvision Enterprises, Inc.

6. What was the name of the architect who hunted "The Invaders"?

Courtesy National Telefilm Associates, Inc.

7. From what valley did "The Real McCoys" migrate to their California farm?

Courtesy Wrather Corporation.

8. Who played "Sergeant Preston of the Yukon"?

9. On what ship did Beanie and Cecil sail?

Courtesy Worldvision Enterprises, Inc.

10. Who starred as Johnny Yuma—"The Rebel"?

"Maverick"

Answers on pages 212–13

(1957–62)

1. According to the show's opening theme song, what was Maverick's companion and what was his game?

2. The antithesis of the hard-riding, rugged Western cowboy, Maverick was an uncourageous, cowardly cardshark who wilted at the sight of blood—especially his own. What was this atypical cowpoke's first name?

3. In addition to his portrayal of the series' title character, James Garner enacted the role of Maverick's poker-playing "Pappy." What was his name?

4. Matching Maverick scheme-for-scheme and ploy-for-ploy was Diane Brewster in the recurring role as the charming swindler _____.

5. Joining Maverick in his weekly escapades later in the series was his scheming yet basically honest brother _____.

6. Veteran of popular television series such as "Bourbon Street Beat," "77 Sunset Strip," "The Big Valley," and "Nanny and the Professor," _____ portrayed Maverick's partner, Gentleman Jack Darby.

7. The Mavericks' dapper cousin, Beauregard, mosied onto the scene during the 1960 season. Perhaps better remembered for his "Saintly" role as Simon Templar, _____ starred as the Texas expatriate who fought with valor in the Civil War.

8. A fourth member of the Maverick clan, younger brother _____, hitched up with his scheming kinfolk in their frolicking misadventures in the Old West.

9. A gambler-swindler friend and confidant of the original Maverick brother, "Dandy" _____ was a semi-regular in the series.

10. What was the name of the "77 Sunset Strip" and "F.B.I." series regular who starred as Maverick's devious confederate?

Hometown Folks

Answers on page 213

Find the names of the city locales in which the following series took place in the maze of alphabet jibberish:

1. "A Brighter Day"
2. "Broken Arrow"
3. "Car 54, Where Are You?"
4. "The Charlie Farrell Show"
5. "Sky King"
6. "Duffy's Tavern"
7. "Hennessey"
8. "I Married Joan"
9. "The George Burns and Gracie Allen Show"
10. "My Three Sons"
11. "The Untouchables"
12. "Where's Raymond"
13. "That's My Boy"
14. "Action in the Afternoon"
15. "Zorro"
16. "Empire"
17. "Casey Jones"
18. "The Flying Nun"
19. "Johnny Ringo"
20. "The Rogues"

```
L E I R E B U H K N A S T A L
O G A C I H C O O R N A I G Y
S N Y U B A I D R O O K A R D
A E L L O S N E S A T Y P O E
N W O A G O A K I N A U W V E
G H G U L L C A N E M O Y E S
E O E K R A P T N A Y R B R N
L P I A J T U S C O N E E C Y
E E D V E L A R D I O T F I E
S G N I R P S M L A P R A T R
A R A S E L O A Y T E A T Y E
W O S L N A U J N A S I N O T
U S H R O S S M O R E L A N N
G A Y A R B R O N X O Y S T O
M S L L I H Y L R E V E B E M
```

"The Mickey Mouse Club"

Answers on pages 213–14

(1955–59)

1. How many original Mouseketeers were there?
2. What was the name of the grown-up, redheaded Mouseketeer who hosted the weekday series?

3. The leader of the mouse-eared youngsters was assisted by his jovial, heavy-set adult friend. What was his name?

4. The heartthrob of many pompadoured teeny-boppers in the late fifties, this Mouseketeer later romped among the beach blankets with Frankie Avalon in several youth-oriented, low-budget films. What was the name of this raven-haired Disney protégée?

5. One of the talented Mouseketeers traded in his rodent-eared beanie to become a regular member of Lawrence Welk's musical family. What was the name of this Mouseketeer?

6. Complete the name of each of the following special "Days" enjoyed each week by Cubby, Karen, Doreen, Lonnie, Sharon, and the rest of the Mouseketeer gang:

    Fun with _____ Day
    Talent _____ Day
    Guest _____ Day
    Anything Can _____ Day

7. Appearing on the series were the weekly adventures of two adolescent boys spending the summer at a Western dude ranch. What was the name of this continuing serial that featured former "My Three Sons" co-star Tim Considine and red-haired David Stollery in the title roles?

8. The suspenseful exploits of two amateur teenage detectives were serialized in a mysterious yarn about a missing treasure of gold doubloons. What were the names of the brother-sleuths?

9. What Mouseketeer was featured in the lead role in the serial "Corky and White Shadow"?

10. Pinocchio's pal, Jiminy Cricket, hosted a segment entitled "I'm No Fool," featuring safety lessons in bicycling, swimming, traffic, and vacation hazards, in addition to handling other informative spots (remember E-N-C-Y-C-L-O-P-E-D-I-A!?). What famous vaudeville recording star ("June Night", "Sleepy Time Gal," "When You Wish Upon a Star") provided the voice for this animated cricket?

"The Millionaire"

Answers on page 214

(1955–60)

1. What was the name of the "mysterious billionaire" who had a penchant for giving away a million dollars each week?

2. Why was the real identity of the actor portraying the faceless tycoon never revealed to the viewing public?

3. What was the unusual origin of the wealthy financier's name?

4. Symbolic of his manipulation of the lives of the nouveau riche he spawned, the billionaire recluse was often seen toying with _____ at the outset of an episode prior to his announcing "the next millionaire."

5. What was the name of the eccentric spendthrift's palatial estate?

6. Marvin Miller starred as _____, the philanthropist's "ever faithful executive secretary" who delivered tax-free million-dollar cashier checks to unsuspecting beneficiaries.

7. What was the name of the bank that issued these seven-digit checks?

8. Under what circumstances was a million-dollar recipient required to return the unspent portion of his windfall?

9. What was so unusual about the role the producer's wife, Mrs. Don Fedderson, played in the series?

10. At the height of the show's popularity, an average of two hundred down-and-out viewers wrote in each week with a hard luck tale of woe and a request for a portion of the "loot" that was being doled out. When the million-dollar giveaway finally retired into syndication, the name of the series was changed to _____.

"Mr. Ed"

Answers on pages 214–15

(1961–66)

1. What breed of horse was the four-legged star of the show?
2. Mr. Ed was kept in a stable behind the home of his owners, Wilbur and Carol _____.
3. How did Wilbur acquire Mr. Ed?
4. Wilbur kept his business office in the stable so he could converse easily with Mr. Ed without fear of being overheard by anyone. What type of work did Wilbur do for a living?
5. Besides Wilbur, who else did Mr. Ed speak to?
6. What was the name of the person who took care of grooming Mr. Ed's mane?
7. Who were Wilbur's original neighbors in this Sunday-night family comedy?
8. What was the name of the racehorse they owned?
9. In a change in casting, Wilbur's former commanding officer and his wife moved their trailer into his backyard on a temporary basis prior to finally purchasing the house next door. What were the names of his ex-Air Force C.O. and his spouse?
10. What ex-cowboy film star provided the human voice for Mr. Ed?

"Mr. Peepers"

Answers on page 215

(1952–55)

1. What actor starred as the quiet and reserved junior high school teacher?
2. What subject did shy Mr. Peepers teach?
3. At what school did the timid instructor hold his classes?

4. What was Mr. Peeper's first name?

5. Mr. Peeper's girl friend, the school nurse, became his wife on May 23, 1954. Pat Benoit starred as the blushing bride, _____.

6. Peeper's colleague and best friend at the school was know-it-all teacher, _____.

7. Urbane _____ created the role of this show-off instructor.

8. Marion Lorne appeared in the series as a stuttering English teacher at Peeper's school. What was the name of the elderly faculty member she portrayed?

9. What was the name of the principal at Mr. Peeper's school?

10. Later to play the leading roles in "The Asphalt Jungle" and "The Wackiest Ship in the Army," _____ portrayed the school's athletic coach.

Crossword #6

Answers on page 216

Clues

Across

1. "_____ Day," game show in which contestants performed household tasks

6. "_____ for Tomorrow," daytime soap opera set in the town of Henderson

11. "_____ and She," situation comedy starring Richard Benjamin and Paula Prentiss

126

12. "The _____ Home Show," hosted by Earl Wrightson

13. Jean Carroll, star of "_____ It from Me"

14. "Star _____ the Family," variety series hosted by Morton Downey

16. _____ Hollister, sheriff of "Tombstone Territory"

18. She served as hostess to Carol Channing on "The Big Party"

20. _____ Winchell, noted ventriloquist

21. "_____ Dog," education series featuring Jo Anne Worley, Jonathan Winters, and Woody Allen

23. He played Harry Lime, "The Third Man"

25. Principal of Hamilton High School on early situation comedy (initials)

26. "_____ Yes or No," game show hosted by playwright Moss Hart

28. Compass direction

29. "City" patrolled by Detectives Adam Flint and Mike Parker

31. "A Time _____ Live," soaper starring Patricia Sully as newspaperwoman Julie Byron

32. He played Corporal Randolph Agarn in "F Troop"

36. "It's Always _____," featuring Janis Page in role of a nightclub entertainer

39. Dr. Joe Gannon on "Medical Center"

40. Female panelist on "Masquerade Party"

41. **PHOTO CLUE:** Street-tough black member of police undercover team, "The Mod Squad"

45. She narrated "Paris Cavalcade of Fashion" in 1948

49. "_____ Parade," variety show featuring The Fort Dix Band and Chorus

53. _____ of the Guard," a "Hallmark Hall of Fame" operetta starring Celeste Holm, Alfred Drake, Bill Hayes, and Barbara Cook

55. "_____ You Want to Lead a Band," musical variety series hosted by Sammy Kaye

56. "Today _____ Ours," soap opera set in the town of Bolton

58. She was told to "get her gun" in Irving Berlin's two-hour Broadway musical telecast in 1957 (initials)

59. Her European cousin, Cathy, lived with her in this situation comedy

60. After leaving a popular science fiction series, he briefly appeared as undercover agent Jeff Cable in "Barbary Coast"

63. A farm implement used by Oliver Douglas on "Green Acres"

65. "_____ Comes the Bride," early Du Mont series on which actual weddings took place

66. She closed every show by blowing a kiss to the audience (initials)

67. James Whitmore appeared as attorney Abraham Lincoln Jones in "The _____ and Mister Jones"

68. After making a smash appearance on "Omnibus," he played the *Drummer Man* on a "Kraft Television Theatre" production at the age of eighteen

Down

1. **PHOTO CLUE:** He played Pete Cochran, the son of wealthy parents, a member of "The Mod Squad"
2. "_____ My Boy," situation comedy about a sports-minded father who tries vainly to turn his bookworm son on to athletics
3. Mickey Rooney starred as Mickey Mulligan, page at International Broadcasting Company, in "_____ Mulligan"
4. Paul Newman fought garment industry racketeers in "The Kaiser Aluminum Hour"'s production of *The _____ Jungle*
5. "_____ Time Playhouse," a mid-fifties dramatic anthology series
6. She co-starred opposite Jack Lemmon in the situation comedy "Heaven for Betsy"
7. "_____ Your Vacation," 1954 game show hosted by Johnny Carson
8. Brock Hayden on "The Doctors," soap opera set at Hope Memorial Hospital (initials)
9. Type of show TV viewers are forced to watch from spring to fall
10. Art Linkletter's "_____ Party"
15. What "The Fugitive" did for four years
17. Lawrence Welk's former "Champagne Lady"
19. He alternated with Alan Young as guest star on "The Saturday Night Revue" in 1954
22. Allen Ludden and Robert Earle hosted this "College Bowl"
24. South Pacific adventure series, "Adventures _____ Paradise"
27. _____ Bond, first trailmaster of "Wagon Train"
30. Bald-headed New York cop with a penchant for lollipops
33. What Doctors Kildare and Casey may ask a patient to say
34. Moderator of "What in the World?," a discussion of archaeological origins
35. TV scriptwriter and star of his own situation comedy, Goodman _____
37. "_____ the World Turns," soap opera that premiered in 1956
38. "The _____ Breed," Los Angeles police drama starring Leslie Nielsen
42. "_____ Dickens . . . He's Fenster," co-starring John Astin and Marty Ingels as carpenters
43. To cause or make
44. "The _____ of Mystery," starring Dick Powell as former gambler Willie Dante, proprietor of Dante's Inferno Nightclub
46. Ben Youens' character portrayal on "Coronation Street" (initials)
47. The sloppy member of "The Odd Couple" (initials)
48. Approaches
50. "Truth _____ Consequences," popular game show hosted by Ralph Edwards, Jack Bailey, and Bob Barker
51. Walter Hurley served as host for "_____ Me a Laugh"
52. Gilles Pelletier starred as Corporal Jacques Gagnier in "_____ Canadian Mounted Police"

54. "_____ Time for Sergeants," military sitcom starring Sammy Jackson as Private Will Stockdale

56. _____ Kabbible appeared with Kay Kyser on the latter's "College of Musical Knowledge"

57. "He and _____," situation comedy starring husband-wife team Richard Benjamin and Paula Prentiss

59. What each member of "Hogan's Heroes" was (abbreviation)

61. He portrayed the colonel of the U.S. Army Criminal Investigation Division on "Pentagon Confidential" (initials)

62. Chico's main "Man," _____ Brown

63. **PHOTO CLUE:** Actress who portrayed the only female member of "The Mod Squad," Julie Barnes (initials)

64. City in which "December Bride" took place (abbreviation)

"My Favorite Martian"

Answers on page 216

(1963–66)

1. After crash-landing on foreign soil, a man from Mars takes up residence with an earthling while seeking a way to repair his damaged spacecraft. Who starred as the stranded alien?

2. The Martian assumed the earthly guise of his host's distant Uncle _____ in an effort to protect his true identity.

3. The friendly Martian possessed the strange powers to make himself invisible, levitate objects, and read people's minds. What was his occupation on his home planet?

4. Having a Martian around the house often proved unsettling to earthling Tim O'Hara. What actor starred as the host to this interplanetary space visitor?

5. When he wasn't covering up for his uncle's Martian eccentricities, Tim worked as a _____.

6. What did the Martian quip when confronted for the first time by his earthling roommate in the series' first episode?

7. Tim rented an upstairs flat from the all-too-inquisitive Mrs. _____.

8. Harboring a strong dislike for both Tim and his strange uncle, Alan Hewitt appeared as the landlady's boyfriend, police detective Lieutenant _____.

9. What was the name of the Martian device that could transform animals into human beings?

10. How did this humanlike Man from Mars perform his amazing feats of levitation?

"My Little Margie"

Answers on page 217

(1952–55)

1. Margie shared an apartment with her widower father. What was the name of the hotel where the madcap couple lived?

2. What was the number of their apartment?

3. Although Margie wanted a "nice old comfortable father," her dad preferred pretty girls and country club tennis to a rocking chair and warm milk. What was the name of Margie's dashing, man-about-town dad?

4. Janet Gaynor's co-star in a dozen of Hollywood's early romantic films, veteran actor _____ appeared in the role of Margie's father.

5. What line of work was he in?

6. What was the name of the company he worked for?

7. What position did he hold in his firm?

8. What was his boss's name?

9. What was the name of his steady girl friend?

10. What was the name of the comedienne who created the meddling and frequently disobedient Margie character?

11. What was the irrepressible Margie's last name?

12. How old was Margie?

13. What was the name of her long-standing beau?

14. What was the name of Margie's 83-year-old neighbor?

15. What was the name of the hotel operator in Margie's building?

Courtesy Worldvision Enterprises, Inc.

"The People's Choice"

Answers on page 217

(1955–58)

1. Ex-*Our Gang Comedy* child star _____ tracked various species of wild birds in his role as government naturalist Socrates "Sock" Miller.

2. Sock's conniving girl friend, the mayor's daughter, managed to exert her political influence in getting Sock elected to an important position in the local community. What office did her ornithologist boyfriend hold?

3. The townspeople of _____ City selected the Bureau of Fish and Wildlife employee as "the people's choice" for city office in a write-in ballot.

4. Sock's Aunt _____ lived with him in a trailer camp before her marriage to Mayor Peoples.

5. Sock and his steady girl friend, _____, were secretly married for one year before they finally broke the news to the bride's disapproving father, His Honor the Mayor.

Courtesy Worldvision Enterprises, Inc.

Courtesy Worldvision Enterprises, Inc.

6. Sock shared his tiny trailer with his ex-Marine buddy, _____, while zealously guarding the secret of his elopement with the mayor's daughter.

7. What was the name of Sock's chief political and romantic rival?

8. What was the name of Sock's penniless artist companion?

9. Upstaging most of her fellow human cast members was Sock's droopy-eared basset hound, _____.

10. Providing the on-screen voice for the inner thoughts of Sock's sad-eyed animal friend was one-time radio actress _____.

Dramatic Pause

Answers on page 218

Find the names of the following characters and personalities from dramatic programs in the maze of alphabet jibberish:

1. Social worker Neil Brock on "East Side/West Side"
2. Storyteller-host of "My Favorite Story"
3. The "Man with a Camera"
4. The distaff side of "Mr. and Mrs. North"
5. "The Girl from U.N.C.L.E."
6. "I Spy" undercover agent masquerading as a tennis champion
7. "The Prisoner" 's number
8. "Mr. Novak" 's principal
9. Chief of Surgery at "The Bold Ones" ' Craig Institute
10. "The Third Man"
11. "The Eleventh Hour" 's resident shrink
12. Charleston Club singer on "The Roaring Twenties"
13. Host of "The Verdict Is Yours" courtroom drama
14. Dr. Joe Gannon's "Medical Center" boss
15. "Owen Marshall" 's secretary
16. "Marcus Welby" 's handsome young assistant
17. Horror film star as "Colonel March of Scotland Yard"
18. Thomas Mitchell hosted this "Playhouse"
19. "Climax" host
20. "Combat" 's Lt. Gil Hanley

```
F A B A R M A P R I L O S A P
L I R I E Y I L A S A G O L A
A R O N E E Y A I T R A U T S
K O J E P Y L I M E E N O N O
R O O K O E L L I L D Y O C H
U R V E M E E Y O I R S T H E
F A Y A I N K O G C A H E E N
A R P Y C O S A I J H O S E R
C H I E H A N Y R A I N T R Y
T O N E E C A M O L T T E Y E
E A K E D O Q U I R O I R R L
V S Y T R A U N N C A F E P I
O H A R E B L A S I X O F I K
G O B A S S E T T R E C I N E
H Y E D A E T H O E M C K A Y
```

"Perry Mason"

Answers on pages 218–19

(1957–66)

1. Burly actor _____ starred as the high-powered attorney with the unblemished trial record.

Courtesy CBS.

2. In what city did the bulky attorney practice law?

3. Barbara Hale appeared as Perry's confidential legal secretary, _____

4. Manning the switchboard in the outer-office was Perry's rarely seen receptionist, _____.

5. Mason often contracted the services of a reputable detective agency to gather information about a particular case. What was the name of the trench coated-shamus who did the counselor's undercover work?

6. What was the name of the handsome, grey-haired actor who portrayed Perry's private gumshoe?

7. Squaring off in the courtroom as Perry's legal adversary was luckless District Attorney _____.

8. Formerly a member of Orson Welles's Mercury Theatre troupe, Ray Collins enacted the role of the hard-boiled police lieutenant who frequently chastised Mason for concealing evidence and harboring fugitives from justice. What was the name of this veteran homicide detective?

9. What was the embittered constable's first name?

10. Originally cast as a defendant in an episode of the series, Wesley Lau returned in the recurring role of police Lieutenant _____ when the regular homicide cop was ailing.

Courtesy CBS.

11. During the series' ninth season, John Anderson added his name to the list of police lieutenants who appeared as semi-regular adversaries of "Perry the Perfect." What was the name of the homicide squad lieutenant he portrayed?

12. While Mason was undergoing minor surgery in 1963, lawyer Constance Doyle filled in for the skillful counselor as his courtroom proxy. What legendary motion picture Academy Award-winning actress guest-starred as this lady trial lawyer?

13. How many criminal court cases did Mason lose during his nine-year residency on television?

14. Who created the fictional Perry Mason character?

15. How many color episodes featuring the wily lawyer-sleuth were produced?

"Rawhide"

Answers on pages 219–20

(1959–66)

1. This rugged Western series chronicled the weekly adventures of an 1866 cattle drive en route from Texas to the upper part of the Mississippi Valley. What city did these cowboys depart?

2. What midwestern city were these wranglers headed for?

3. Approximately how many head of cattle were being herded to market in this Friday-night cattle drive?

4. The "hellbent for leather" trail boss commanded the respect of the rough-and-tumble cowboys who rode herd with him. What was the name of the hard-nosed cowpuncher who kept those dogies rollin'?

138

5. The ill-fated actor who "moved 'em up and out" each week drowned while filming a scene for a motion picture. Who was the victim of this tragedy?

6. Next in command along the cattle drive was the boss's hot-headed ramrod, Rowdy Yates. What popular "spaghetti Western" movie idol portrayed this raw-boned steerherder?

7. Paul Brinegar listened to many grumbles and complaints about the quality of the daily chow he served in his role as the cook, _____.

8. Assisting the trail-herd cook in his culinary duties was an empty-headed cowpoke played by James Murdock. What was the unusual nickname of the chef's helper?

9. Perhaps best-remembered for his recording of the rock 'n' roll hit "Purple People Eater," _____ portrayed the cattle drive's scout, Pete Nolan.

10. What famous recording artist belted out the theme song for this Western saga?

"The Rifleman"

Answers on page 220

(1958–63)

1. Chuck Connors portrayed widower _____ in his title role as the Rifleman.

2. What professional basketball team did Connors once play for?

3. What type of rifle did the ex-Brooklyn Dodger farmhand use to dispose of weekly villains?

4. What was the name of the Rifleman's respectful and dutifully obedient son?

5. Before playing the Rifleman's son, _____ appeared as a Mouseketeer on "The Mickey Mouse Club."

6. In what New Mexico town did the Rifleman and his son reside?

7. Marshal _____ was responsible for upholding the peace in this Western hamlet.

8. After Hattie Denton left town, the local general store was operated by "Miss Millie" _____.

Courtesy Four Star Entertainment Corporation.

Courtesy Four Star Entertainment Corporation.

Courtesy Four Star Entertainment Corporation.

9. What was the name of the prairie town's schoolteacher?
10. A beautiful red-haired saloon keeper (shades of Miss Kitty!) arrived in town from Denver and sparked a touch of romance in the Rifleman's loveless life. What was the name of "Paw"'s new lady friend?

"The Roy Rogers Show"

Answers on page 221

(1951–57)

1. The "King of the Cowboys" teamed with his wife, _____, in combating black-hatted desperados on this weekly series.
2. What was the name of the "Queen of the West"'s trusty steed?
3. What was the name of Roy's golden palomino?
4. Roy's "wonder dog" was a fleet German Shepherd named _____.

141

5. Providing the comedy relief on these action-filled programs was Roy's sidekick, _____.

6. What did Roy's slaphappy pal do for a living?

7. Roy's bungling companion drove a jeep whose side door bore its name— _____.

8. What was the slapstick comic's unusual middle name?

9. Roy and his wife lived on a modest-sized ranch located on the outskirts of Mineral City. What was the name of their spread?

10. The show ended each week on a musical note with Roy and his wife singing their closing theme song, "_____."

Crossword #7

Photo Courtesy Worldvision Enterprises, Inc.

Answers on page 221

Clues

Across

1. His wife, Lois, along with orchestra leader Milton DeLugg, appeared with him on his early 50's variety series

9. _____-73, "McHale's Navy" 's boat

10. He portrayed Terrence, "Wonderful John Action" 's brother (initials)

11. "Stop_____ If You've Heard This One," game show on which comedians supplied punch lines to jokes
12. Claude _____ starred in "The Kaiser Aluminum Hour" 's presentation of *Antigone*
14. Singing star of "The Lively Ones"
15. Gene Kelly starred as Father Charles O'Malley in the comedy-drama series "_____ My Way"
17. Nickname of Richard Boone's Deputy Ramsey role
19. WAVE Molly McGuire on "Broadside" (initials)
20. What "Adam-12" used on its way to an emergency
23. Eddie Mayehoff starred as dentist "_____ _____"
25. Final contestants on "Let's Make a Deal" were asked to select from one of three _____
26. Robert Ripley hosted "Believe It _____ Not"
27. Tactical police unit headed by Steve Forrest as Lieutenant Hondo Harrelson
29. Monte Markham was unearthed after being frozen alive for a century on "The Second Hundred _____"
32. Herb Shriner and Sam Levenson hosted the game show "Two _____ the Money"
34. Researcher Glenn Barton on "The Man and the Challenge"
35. **PHOTO CLUE:** _____ Starke played Toby, one of the pictured star's children, on her television series
36. Contestants connected fifty dots to form the face of a mystery celebrity on this game show
37. University of Michigan All-American who broadcast many football telecasts (initials)
39. He combined with David Niven and Charles Boyer to form "The Rogues"
42. Thomas Mitchell hosted dramatizations of this famous author's works on an anthology "Playhouse" series
44. "_____ Bad Girl," starring Patty McCormack as preteen Torey
47. Patrick _____ appeared in the cast of *Caesar and Cleopatra*, a 1956 "Producers' Showcase" play
49. "Try and Do _____," a game show played on picnic grounds
50. He played Terry Lee on "Terry and the Pirates"
51. William Russell played the swordsman-knight "_____ Lancelot"
53. Ozzie, Harriet, Ricky, and David
55. "What's Going _____?," game show pitting the Insiders against the Outsiders
56. Senior editor Dan Farrell on "The Name of the Game"
58. He was "Pip the Piper"
59. Mingo, "Daniel Boone" 's Cherokee Indian companion

Down

1. **PHOTO CLUE:** Blonde motion picture star who appeared in her own situation comedy on television
2. Cesar Romero as courier Steve McQuinn in "Passport to _____"
3. This rock 'n' roll star's three appearances on Ed Sullivan's show earned him $50,000 (initials)
4. Johnny Mann's "_____ Up and Cheer"
5. Ida Lupino played Howard Duff's wife on "Mr. Adams and _____"
6. Space "Captain" played by Al Hodge, who was "The Guardian of the Safety of the World"
7. Johnny Carson's long-time announcer (initials)
8. Soap opera, "The _____ Storm"
11. **PHOTO CLUE:** _____ Valley, California, setting for this leading lady's sitcom
13. Family situation comedy, "My Three _____"
16. Larry Hagman as architect Richard Evans in the comedy series, "Here We _____ Again"
17. A famous composer, he starred as Jonesy in "Laramie" (initials)
18. What Mary Martin sang "I Gotta" do in "Peter Pan"
21. Two of the vowels
22. Anthology series, "_____ Interlude"
24. Company that hosted a "Music Hall," "Mystery Theatre," "Suspense Theatre," and "Television Theatre"
27. The _____ Brothers, Dick and Tommy
28. Tomboy Pamela Blake in "_____ Young to Go Steady"
30. Self-esteem
31. "_____ Playhouse," anthology series originally aired as "Schlitz Playhouse of Stars"
33. He played Jerry, the hubby, on "Mr. and Mrs. North" (initials)
36. Anthology series "The _____ Show of the Month" later appeared as a weekly series
38. "_____ Haw," country-western variety series co-hosted by Buck Owens and Roy Clark
40. She roamed the jungle in a shorty leopard suit as "Sheena, Queen of the Jungle" (initials)
41. Frequent talk-show guest, diamond-studded Zsa Zsa _____
42. "_____ Happy Family," sitcom starring Dick Sargent as Dick Cooper
43. Belonging to actor who appeared in "Playhouse 90" 's productions of *Last Clear Chance* and *The Time of Your Life*
45. _____ *Me Kate*, Cole Porter musical telecast as a 1958 "Hallmark Hall of Fame" production
46. "Bus _____," dramatic series set in Sunrise, Colorado

48. Where "Top Cat" lived
51. "_____ Benedict," courtroom dramas starring Edmond O'Brien
52. "The _____ Palace," variety series featuring skaters
54. Title of series featuring the trials and tribulations of newsmen, hosted by Hal Burdick (initials)
57. Captain Greer on "The Mod Squad" (initials)

"77 Sunset Strip"

Answers on page 222

(1958–64)

1. _____ was featured each week as Stuart Bailey, the ex-O.S.S. officer who anchored the high-powered detective firm.

2. Handsome actor-director Roger Smith tooled around town in his white T-Bird while on the trail of mysterious suspects and in the service of intriguing female clients. What was the name of the suave gumshoe he portrayed in this fast-paced, action-packed Warner Brothers' series?

3. What vivacious singer-dancer is Mr. Smith's real-life wife?

4. Originally cast as a psychopathic killer in the series' first episode, Edward Byrnes was later injected into the show in a continuing role as the neighboring club's offbeat parking lot attendant. What was the name of this groovy cat?

5. Baby — you're the ginchiest! Aside from popularizing the beat lingo of the 50's, this groovy carhop cut a record on which Connie Stevens provided the backup voice. What was the name of the platter he waxed?

6. What type of $8,000 customized auto did the wavy-haired teen idol drive?

7. What was the name of the club where he worked?

8. Although he was known to millions of viewers by his nickname, this "cool" parking lot hustler's full name was _____.

9. During the show's fourth season on television, the groovy car-jockey traded in his car keys for a new assignment. What was it?

10. Always using letters to abbreviate his words (GAN—Good As New), young _____ replaced America's favorite parking lot attendant as the new "CP" (Car Parker).

11. In between trips to the $2 betting window at the local racetrack, friendly neighborhood horse player _____ joined in the confab at the private investigators' Sunset Strip hangout.

12. What actor provided the show's comic relief as this cigar-chewing ex-Broadway bettor?

13. What was the name of the boys' sexy, long-legged receptionist-secretary?

14. What was the one-client business she operated on the side in addition to playing secretary to the detectives?

15. The Hollywood detective firm gained a new partner later in the series when shamus Rex Randolph changed venue from his familiar down-South "Beat" to the West Coast city. What series did Randolph leave in order to link up with the Sunset Strip gang?

16. What veteran television actor portrayed this transplanted New Orleans private cop?

17. In 1963, Joan Staley made her entrance into the investigators' lair as Stu Bailey's secretary, _____.

18. Which one of the Hollywood investigators held a Ph.D. in philosophy from an Ivy League university?

19. What was the name of the police lieutenant who rounded up the guilty parties at show's end?

20. Only one member of the original cast of Sunset Strip regulars was on hand for the start of the program's sixth season on prime-time television. Who was this lone survivor of the detective firm?

"The $64,000 Question"

Answers on pages 222–23

(1955–58)

1. Former co-star with Tom D'Andrea in the short-lived service comedy "The Soldiers," debonair _____ acted as the show's quizmaster.

2. What was the name of the attractive hostess who introduced contestants to the show's emcee?

3. The first four questions posed to a contestant were fed to the show's master of ceremonies by an _____. If answered successfully, the remaining questions were brought on stage by Ben Feit, Manufacturers Trust executive. Flanked by two bank guards, Mr. Feit informed the audience that all questions used on the program were compiled by a scholarly Board of Educators. He then proceeded to perform his weekly ritual of delivering the following spiel:

> All questions come from the locked vault of Manufacturers Trust . . . Manufacturers Trust guarantees that only authorized members of the bank have the keys and combinations of the vault . . . and except for the editors, no one has seen these questions . . . not even myself.

4. Once a contestant accumulated $4,000 in winnings, he was guaranteed the gift of a _____, even if he lost his earnings on a return visit to the show.

5. Perspiring contestants grappled for correct answers while inside sound-proof enclosures called _____.

6. Many celebrities tried their hand at answering big-money questions over a wide variety of subject areas. Singer Nancy Wilson ironically missed the $64,000 question in the Pop Music category while Jack Benny decided to "retire" with the $64 he earned answering questions about the violin. Unlike his contemporaries, however, legendary horror film star Boris Karloff managed to win $16,000. What was the subject Karloff mastered in amassing his winnings?

7. What was the name of the now-famous psychologist whose extensive knowledge of boxing resulted in her winning the grand prize of $64,000?

8. What was the name of the ten-year-old whiz kid who mastered the fine points of science to collect $64,000 in prize money in 1957?

9. What was the name of the Burford, Georgia grandmother who took home a wheelbarrow full of money by conquering the category of baseball?

10. What was the name of the diminutive jockey who pocketed a fortune in prize money by correctly answering questions about art, only to lose it many years later in the Las Vegas gambling casinos?

11. What was the name of the little old shoemaker who rattled off answers to impossible questions on opera en route to winning thousands of dollars in prize money?

12. What was the name of the bespectacled supply clerk with the photographic memory who dropped out of school at thirteen yet walked away with the top prize on this big-money giveaway?

13. Who was the "authority's authority" for all the brain-teasing questions used on this program?

14. What cosmetic company sponsored the program?

15. Former co-star to Richard Denning in the comedy-mystery series "Mr. and Mrs. North," _____ was commercial spokeswoman for products advertised on the program.

Who Was That Masked Man?

Answers on page 223

Find the names of the following characters and personalities from Western programs in the maze of alphabet jibberish:

1. The Cisco Kid's happy-go-lucky amigo
2. Gene Autry's trusty horse
3. Cheyenne's surname
4. "Wagon Train" 's first trailmaster
5. Bounty hunter Josh Randall
6. Kit Carson's Mexican sidekick
7. Gene Barry wielded a cane as this dapper frontier lawman
8. "Big Valley" matriarch
9. "Branded" Army captain falsely accused of cowardice
10. "Zane Grey Theatre" performer-host
11. Southpaw-shootin' Wells Fargo agent
12. "The Tall Man" 's gunfighter friend
13. "Wichita Town" Marshal Mike Dunbar
14. Don Diego de la Vega's secret masked rider guise
15. John Payne's "Restless Gun" role
16. The McLaughlin family's beloved stallion
17. "The Law West of the Pecos"
18. Foreman of Garrett Ranch "Empire"
19. Family name of "High Chaparral" clan
20. "Brave, courageous, and bold" Marshal Wyatt Earp

```
P R O T H A U R E N N O B C A
L A I R O T C I V Y E O L A S
O W N A C R O N E E D R A N T
K E E C A H O D R I Y O N N E
R A F O H O R I E C A T O O N
A D E N O O R A W O L L A N O
Y A M E C H O D E N A E B O I
S M O C I O Z E R U L I R O P
E S M I Q U E F F A L O B Y M
I M C R U U S O O L A R L E A
D O C H A S E K Y M I L O C H
R A R E B A G E S A N C A I C
A R E D I G O A N I T O K R E
H E A R O L A P O W E L L A D
E D R O V E T A W S E L I N E
```

"Star Trek"

Answers on page 224

(1966–69)

1. A space vessel and its 430-member crew embarked on an exploratory mission spanning the vast horizons of several distant galaxies. For how many years was the starship scheduled to remain on its venture into the frontiers of space?

2. In what century did these space age explorations take place?

3. The spacecraft's persevering captain occupied a top-level position in the Space Service as Commander of a United States starship. What was the name of the resourceful leader of the international crew of space explorers?

4. What was the name of the colossal-sized starship he commanded?

5. What was the Registry Number of the powerful military starship?

6. What was the name of the space vessel's seven-seat shuttlecraft?

7. What was the name of the first captain of the 190,000-ton vessel?

8. The ship's Science Officer was the product of a mixed-marriage between an earth woman and a native from the nonsolar planet of Vulcan. What was the name of the logical-thinking half-man, half-alien who was second-in-command aboard the starship?

9. The half-breed alien's diplomat-physicist father was named Sarek. Who was his schoolteacher mother?

10. Relying on his superior intellect, the pointy-eared alien subdued enemy attackers by applying pressure to an extremely vulnerable part of his adversary's body. Where did the ship's First Officer apply his paralyzing Vulcan pinch?

11. Whenever a crew member fell ill or was injured in combat, he was rushed to Sick Bay for treatment by the ship's surgeon, Dr. _____.

12. By what anatomical nickname was the spacecraft's physician more commonly known?

13. The ship's chief nurse, Christine Chapel, harbored a deep affection for one of the crew members. Do you remember which one?

14. The Communications Officer aboard the starship was an impassive Bantu woman named _____.

15. The ship's Chief Engineer was a volatile technician of European extraction. What was his ethnic-sounding nickname?

16. Most of the starship's critical engine circuitry was located in the _____ Tube.

17. Ensign _____ was the spacecraft's slender Russian navigator.

18. Steady as she goes! Sharing the bridge with the ship's captain was the crew's Oriental chief pilot. What was the name of the helmsman who also served as Chief Weapons Officer?

19. Whose secondary bridge function was it to maintain control over the starship's library-computer?

20. When fleeing from the danger of an enemy attack, the ship's captain would order his pilot to quickly retreat at _____ speed.

21. What type of pistol-like weapons did crew members use to defend themselves against their Romulan and Klingon enemies?

22. What was the name of the mechanical devices used by crew members to gather data on the nature and substance of life forms?

23. Always carried by one or more landing party members, the _____ was a combination portable sensor-computer recording device that was capable of measuring, analyzing, and storing information on all subject matter.

24. What was the name of the device that enabled the ship's transporter to locate, lock on, and "beam aboard" any member of the crew?

25. Captain's Log...Star Date 1984. Years after the series' departure from the airwaves, avid fans have organized themselves to protest the cancellation of the program and to exchange nostalgic remembrances and memorabilia about the spacecraft's voyages. What are these enclaves of loyal and vociferous "Star Trek" worshippers called?

"The Steve Allen Show"

Answers on pages 224–25

(1956–59)

1. What perennial hit series was broadcast opposite Steve's variety program on a rival network?

2. Later the host of the popular television game show, "The Match Game," _____ handled the announcing chores on Steve's show.

3. What husband-wife singing duo was featured as regulars on the program?

4. The show's "Man-on-the-Street" comedy-interview routine became a show biz classic. Who appeared as the visibly nervous streetside interviewee?

5. What was this high-strung passerby's standard response to the question, "Are you nervous?"

6. Who portrayed Man-on-the-Street Gordon Hathaway, a debonair blade from Manhattan?

7. What was his familiar greeting to Steve?

8. What was Man-on-the-Street Tom Poston always forgetting?

9. Name Steve's bearded bandleader who sometimes joined the Man-on-the-Street entourage as the "Man from the Bronx"?

10. What funnyman created the character of the lovable, sad-eyed Latin, José Jiminez?

"Texaco Star Theater"

Answers on page 225

(1948–56)

1. Lavish production numbers, outlandish costumes, and raucous comedy were the trademarks of this extremely popular weekly variety extravaganza. Millions of rabid fans remained home on _____ nights to watch the zany Berle perform his sidesplitting comedy routines.

2. A pioneer of early television programming, Milton Berle was appropriately known as Mr. _____.

3. What was the television pioneer's most famous and often repeated catchphrase?

4. Milton became a familiar household figure as the show's master of ceremonies. Feeling an intimate relationship with his millions of adoring fans, Berle adopted the kindred nickname of _____ Miltie.

5. Fill in the missing amount in the classic Berle one-liner: "I'll kill you a _____ times!"

6. What is the name of the nasal-voiced, scrawny comedian of Chunky "chawclate" commercial fame who played Berle's stagehand, Francis?

7. Appearing as Berle's squeaky-voiced secretary in many hilarious sketches was the ever popular _____.

8. What was the masculine-sounding name of the character she portrayed?

9. What was the famous catchphrase of the show's pitchman, Sid Stone?

10. Ventriloquist _____ and his dummy _____ hawked Texaco products in between the fast and furious slapstick comedy on the show.

Crossword #8

Photo Courtesy Worldvision Enterprises, Inc.

Answers on page 226

Clues

Across

1. **PHOTO CLUE:** She dressed up in a chicken suit on Rowan and Martin's zany comedy series

10. Bert Convy played Lt. _____ _____, nephew of "The Snoop Sisters," a segment of the "NBC Wednesday Mystery Movie" (initials)

12. _____ O'Neal, a member of the Garrett family on "Empire"

13. She appeared with Harry Belafonte on "Tonight with Belafonte" in 1959
15. Belonging to the one-armed ex-gunslinger portrayed by David McLean
16. "_____ Pays to Be Married," quiz show hosted by Bill Goodwin
17. Richard Willis provided beauty tips to women on "_____ Your Best"
18. What they did with the $25,000 cash grand prize on "Treasure Hunt"
20. "_____ in a Suitcase," starring Richard Bradford as John McGill
21. "Broadway _____ House," late-night variety series hosted by Jerry Lester
25. "Clutch _____," animated cartoon series
26. Rear Admiral Ray Foster Brown narrated the British naval series "_____ War"
28. "The _____'s the Same," hosted by Robert Q. Lewis, Dennis James, and Bob & Ray
29. Clean-cut rock 'n' roll balladeer who was once a member of Arthur Godfrey's cast
31. Michael _____ starred opposite Margot Fonteyn in the "Producers' Showcase" presentation of *The Sleeping Beauty*
33. "The Price _____ Right," game show on which contestants guess the value of prizes
34. Ronald Winters starred in "Doorway _____ Danger"
35. Actor Alan _____
36. _____ Brown and His Band of Renown
37. Now a top motion picture star, he played Rodney Harrington on the serial "Peyton Place" (initials)
38. Grace Kelly starred in the "Studio One" production *The* _____
40. He and his wife took in two college coeds in their short-lived second TV sitcom
44. Rank of Rip Riddle on "The Wackiest Ship in the Army" (abbreviation)
46. Red Foley hosted the country-western musical variety series "_____ Jubilee"
47. Miss Williams on "Laverne and Shirley"
52. The Lone Ranger made his bullets out of silver found in his _____
53. Ben Casey's superior, Dr. Zorba
54. "_____ Tonight," an anthology series featuring television newcomers
56. _____ Zimbalist, Inspector Erskine on "The F.B.I."
57. Helen Hayes made her TV debut in "Pulitzer Prize Playhouse"'s production of *The* _____ *Christopher Bean*
59. Perry Como's announcer (initials)
60. "Act _____ Out," game show on which scenes were acted out by performers and answered by home viewers
62. Type of animal the animated Magilla was
64. One competes against another on many game shows

66. **PHOTO CLUE:** This actress played the switchboard operator on the same Rowan and Martin series featuring the pictured star
67. Sammy _____ set the play *Our Town* to music with James Van Heusen on "Producers' Showcase"
68. Johnny Carson's "Tea Time Movie" host, _____ Fern

Down

1. Space-age family featured in an animated sitcom
2. Messrs. Carney, James, and Linkletter
3. Louis _____ played Dr. Delbert Gray, the house doctor of the Bartley House Hotel on "The Ann Sothern Show"
4. "_____ Airflyte Theatre," anthology series hosted by William Gaxton
5. Dr. Michael Ross on "Peyton Place" (initials)
6. "Captain Video," "Captain Midnight," and "Captain Z-Ro" took place in _____ space
7. The Goldbergs ate this with cream cheese and bagels
8. _____ Wynn played John Beamer, a retired businessman trying to raise two orphaned granddaughters in a comedy series
9. Shirley _____, Charley on "The Lively Ones"
10. Messrs. Sid, Milburn, and Harvey
11. Type of tree Smokey tried to protect along with other flora and fauna on "The Smokey the Bear Show," an animated series
14. "_____ of the Town," Ed Sullivan's variety series
16. Miss Lupino
19. She played the maid "Grindl" in a situation comedy (initials)
22. Countess Christina _____ appeared on "Mr. Broadway," starring Craig Stevens
23. _____ Simpson played Katherine Squire on "The Doctors"
24. Want or desire
27. "_____ Burke, Secret Agent," starring Gene Barry
29. Select or choose
30. Mrs. Phillips on "The Bill Dana Show" (initials)
32. The puppeteer on "Judy Splinters" (initials)
34. "_____ It to Groucho," a quiz-interview program hosted by Mr. Marx
36. He appeared with his orchestra-leader brother Guy on the latter's "Diamond Jubilee" musical variety series (initials)
37. "_____ for One More," sitcom starring Andrew Duggan as engineer George Rose
39. **PHOTO CLUE:** "Laugh-_____," series on which pictured comedienne appeared as a regular
41. Western anthology series, "Dick Powell's _____ Grey Theatre"

42. Full of anger
43. Trend-setting comic who was married to Edie Adams at the time of his tragic death (initials)
45. "_____: The Corrupters," starring Stephen McNally and Robert Harland as undercover operatives
47. "_____ Runamuck," starring Arch Johnson as Commander Wivenhoe
48. Peggy McKay played this nurse on "General Hospital" (initials)
49. "_____ Monday Night Football," featuring Howard Cosell
50. Stanley Andrews narrated "_____ Valley Days" as "The Old Ranger"
51. "The _____ Liberty Club," featuring Jacqueline as the musical variety series' hostess
53. As Patricia Marshall, _____ Arthur worked for the law firm of Marshall and Marshall on a situation comedy
54. Lloyd Bridges did most of his acting under this in his classic role of Mike Nelson
55. "Air Time," a musical variety series presented by the U.S. _____ Reserve (abbreviation)
58. Including host Peter Marshall, the number of "stars" on "The Hollywood Squares" game show
60. "_____ Was a Very Good Year," nostalgia series hosted by singer Mel Tormé
61. "_____ Rome with Love," starring John Forsythe as widower Michael Endicott
63. Banjo-eyed comic who helped pioneer television with his appearances on "The Colgate Comedy Hour" (initials)
65. Relationship of Ida to Rhoda Morganstern

"The Today Show"

Answers on page 226

(1952–Present)

1. Who was the original host of the dawn-breaking program that has been both informing and entertaining millions of early-rising Americans for over a quarter of a century?
2. The bespectacled host's traditional sign-off consisted of an upraised palm and the accompanying one-word slogan "_____."

3. The Features Editor on the early morning gabfest was an ex-Columbia University professor who gained notoriety from his complicity in the television quiz show scandals. What was the name of the Ivy League prof who was "coached" while a contestant on "Twenty-One"?

4. Formerly a panelist on "I've Got a Secret," _____ preceded Florence Henderson, Helen O'Connell, and Barbara Walters in the coveted role as Woman's Editor on the program.

5. Predecessor to dome-topped Joe Garagiola and his behind-the-plate baseball witticisms was the series' original Sports Editor, _____.

6. The only remaining carry-over from the original cast, _____ retired as the show's long-time News Editor.

7. A frequent visitor to the program was a playful chimpanzee who often upstaged members of the cast. What was the name of the clever monkey who was once accused of biting members of "The Today Show" entourage?

8. After allegedly biting the hand that was feeding him, the rambunctious chimp was summarily fired by the network. How did the deposed animal star retaliate?

9. How did New Yorkers standing outside the studio say hello to television audiences from coast to coast each weekday morning?

10. A former sidekick of Jack Paar and master of ceremonies of the long-running game show "Concentration," _____ served as host of "The Today Show" for a record nine years.

"Topper"

Answers on page 227

(1953-56)

1. Topper was the sedate banker who was "haunted" by the presence of a ghostly couple and their martini-drinking dog. According to the show's weekly introduction, Anne Jeffreys appeared as _____ Kirby, "the ghostess with the mostest," and Robert Sterling appeared as _____ Kirby, "that most haunting spirit."

2. Veteran motion picture actor _____ starred as the reluctant "host to said ghosts" in his role as Topper.

3. What was Topper's rather unusual first name?

4. What was the name of the Kirbys' alcoholic canine?

5. What type of dog was he?

6. How did the Kirbys and their pet meet their untimely demise?

7. What year anniversary was the ghostly couple marking on the day they met their doom?

8. Topper was a pillar of the financial community. What was the name of the bank where he worked?

9. What position did Topper hold at the bank?

10. Topper's boss was the bank's blustery president, Mr. _____.

11. In what city did Topper live?

12. Unable to detect the Kirbys' presence, the Toppers' maid, _____, was often mystified by floating objects around the house.

13. Lee Patrick starred as Topper's emotional and incredibly naive spouse, _____.

14. Aside from Topper, who else could see and hear the ghostly trio?

15. Why did the ghostly trio choose to haunt the Topper family's home?

"What's My Line?"

Answers on page 227

(1950–67)

1. Who were the four original panelists on this pioneer quiz show?

2. The articulate quizmaster of "What's My Line?" was a former ABC newsman and vice-president. Who was this distinguished host?

3. What was the prim-and-proper moderator's middle name?

4. Anchoring the panel and wearing her familiar heart-shaped diamond pendant was the insightful _____.

5. Rounding out the trio of regular panelists was Random House publisher _____ and columnist _____.

6. What was the unusual occupation of the first guest to appear on the program?

7. Before taking a seat, all contestants were required to perform a certain ritual. What was it?

8. Panelists donned their blindfolds when trying to guess the identity of the _____ Challenger.

9. Who was the first unseen celebrity guest to challenge the panel to guess his secret identity?

10. Mark _____ and Bill _____ acted as co-producers for this, the granddaddy of all television quiz shows.

More Canned Laughter

Answers on page 228

Find the names of the following characters and personalities from situation comedies in the maze of alphabet jibberish:

1. "The Addams Family" 's gargantuan butler
2. Perplexed grocery store owner on "Dennis the Menace"
3. "The Farmer's Daughter"—Katy Holstrum
4. Jewish family residing at 1030 East Tremont Avenue, Apartment 3-B, Bronx, New York
5. Councilman-farmer Sam Jones's son on "Mayberry R.F.D."
6. Nurse "Julia" 's crabby boss
7. Mrs. Muir's ghostly boarder
8. Muldoon's dumpy-looking squad-car partner on "Car 54, Where Are You?"
9. Dagwood on first TV version of "Blondie"
10. Domestic portrayed by Ethel Waters, Hattie McDaniel, and Louise Beavers
11. Sister "The Flying Nun" Betrille's first name
12. Gomer Pyle's singer-girl friend
13. Navy doctor Lt. Chick "Hennessey"
14. Distaff side of "He and She"
15. Teenage niece of "Bachelor Father"
16. "Pete and Gladys" ' last name
17. "Life with Father" 's turn-of-the-century family
18. Japanese housekeeper on "The Courtship of Eddie's Father"
19. Reincarnated mom's voice on "My Mother the Car"
20. "That Girl"

```
A L M A D O C E G A D D Y O P
C O O P E R E E R R E Y A L E
H A C I E Y N P A D E E M R A
O C A T H N O R I Y N G O U N
A R R O A O K A M E S O G R G
S O N U B E U L A H U E E M O
P L O X L E N A R U I H E A L
A L A L I V I N G S T O N I D
U A Y E S O B E L O A N U L B
L I D E T D E E S Y M E J U E
A F O G E R E X O A E E Y N R
T R O A V E N O R I S K U I G
O U T Y E L G I U Q U I A T S
P R A I N E E N Y U M M O L E
L D B E S H E Y E L G E H C E
```

"You Bet Your Life"

Answers on page 228

(1950–61)

1. Cigar-puffing Groucho Marx acted as the wisecracking host of this comedy-quiz program. What standard line did he employ when greeting new contestants to the show?

2. If a contestant mentioned the night's pre-selected "secret word" during his conversation with Groucho, a strange-looking creature would drop down from overhead with the word tied around his neck and a cash prize for the lucky game-player. What type of animal brought the good news to unsuspecting contestants?

3. What was the name of the pretty young lass who replaced this animal messenger by descending in a swing seat to hand-deliver cash to contestants who spoke the secret word in conversation with Groucho?

4. How much money did a contestant win if he was lucky enough to say the secret word?

5. What did a contestant-team win if they correctly answered four questions in succession?

6. How many missed questions in a row eliminated a contestant-team?

7. Winning couples could come back at the end of the show to try their luck at increasing their earnings. What was the top prize they could earn?

8. Consolation prizes were easily won when apparent losers came up with the obvious answer to the ludicrous question, "_____."

9. At the conclusion of each program, Groucho urged listeners to visit his sponsor's automobile showroom and remember to tell them _____.

10. Groucho's announcer, _____, was often on the receiving end of the quipster's one-line barbs.

"You'll Never Get Rich"

Answers on page 229

(1955–59)

1. _____ was a multiple Emmy winner for his portrayal of the lovable Army shyster, Sergeant Ernest Bilko.

2. The scheming Bilko and his platoon cronies were stationed at an out-of-the-way base in Kansas. What was the name of this obscure Army camp?

3. In what midwestern city was this U.S. Army outpost located?

4. The wheeler-dealer Master Sergeant and his motley crew of the Third Platoon of Company B were assigned to the _____ at the base.

Courtesy CBS.

5. Bilko's get-rich-quick schemes placed him at loggerheads with the pudgy commandant of the unmilitary-like Army installation. What was this long-suffering colonel's name?

6. What was the name of the base commander's wife?

7. One of Bilko's merry men later appeared as a sensitive police captain in the weekly crime drama "Mod Squad." What was the name of this veteran actor who also appeared as a flatfoot in Robert Taylor's "The Detectives"?

8. The all-time goldbrick artist's two stooge-like henchmen were Corporals Henshaw and Rocco _____.

9. The fast-talking platoon leader once remarked that the moon-faced patsy of his squad looked like an "unmade bed." What was this sappy-looking private's name?

10. Elizabeth Fraser appeared as Bilko's pretty blonde WAC girl friend, Master Sergeant _____.

11. Perhaps best remembered for his caricatured portrayal of a bumbling police officer in the short-lived police spoof "Car 54, Where Are You?," Joe E. Ross played Mess Sergeant _____, the "Lucretia Borgia" of Company B.

12. What was the name of the cook's wife?

13. One of the most hilarious episodes in the show's history involved the platoon leader's defense of a chimpanzee draftee who was mistakenly inducted into the service. What was the name of this hairy recruit?

14. Bilko never minded "walking a mile" for his cigarette sponsor (if he had, he'd have been out of a job!). What was the name of the original company that brought you these zany Army misadventures?

15. Who was the ingenious creator-writer of this service comedy?

Photo Quiz #3

Answers on page 229

Courtesy National Telefilm Associates, Inc.

1. Where did Steve Wilson ply his trade as a crusading crime reporter?

2. Who was "Underdog" 's sweetheart?

3. Who played Diablo's resident markswoman, Annie Oakley?

Courtesy Worldvision Enterprises, Inc.

4. Who portrayed Lt. Gil Hanley of K Company on "Combat"?

Courtesy Worldvision Enterprises, Inc.

5. What is Liberace's full name?

6. Who is playing the piano in Yogi Bear's band?
7. What was the name of the Oriental houseboy who assisted the Green Hornet (left) in his daring crime-fighting exploits?

Courtesy Greenway Productions.

Courtesy Richard Webb Productions.

8. What was the name of the Secret Squadron commander known to millions of adoring kids as "Captain Midnight"?

9. Who starred as Colin "Glencannon" (second from left)?

Courtesy National Telefilm Associates, Inc.

Courtesy Worldvision Enterprises, Inc.

10. What macho motion picture star once portrayed free lance photographer Mike Kovac, the "Man with a Camera"?

Answers

Answers—"The Abbott and Costello Show"

1. Who's on First
2. *The Naughty Nineties*
3. "Jazz Babies' Ball"
4. Bud Abbott and Lou Costello
5. Actors
6. Sidney Fields
7. Stinky
8. Joe Besser
9. Hillary Brooke
10. Mike (Gordon Jones)
11. Mr. Bacciagalupe (Joe Kirk)
12. An undersized derby
13. Bingo
14. He dressed exactly like Lou
15. "I'm a b-a-a-d boy!"

Answers—"The Amos 'n' Andy Show"

1. Kingfish (Tim Moore)
2. Brown (Spencer Williams, Jr.)
3. "Hog"
4. Sapphire (Ernestine Wade)
5. The Hall of the Mystic Knights of the Sea
6. Lightning (Nick Stuart)
7. Fresh Air
8. Ruby (Jane Adams)

9. Andy

10. Miss Genevieve Blue (Madaline Lee)

11. New York City

12. Queen (Lillian Randolph)

13. She was a singer

14. Algonquin J. Calhoun (Johnny Lee)

15. "The Perfect Song"

Answers—"The Andy Griffith Show"

1. Andy Taylor

2. He was the editor of the town newspaper and justice of the peace

3. Opie (Ronny Howard)

4. Bee

5. Frances Bavier

6. Mayberry

7. Barney B. Fife

8. Don Knotts

9. In the breast pocket of his shirt

10. Thelma Lou (Betty Lynn)

11. 596

12. Mrs. Mendelbright (Enid Markey)

13. Warren Ferguson (Jack Burns)

14. Elinor Donahue

15. Floyd Lawson (Howard McNear)

16. Peggy (Joanna Moore)

17. Jim Nabors

18. Wally

19. Goober Pyle (George Lindsey)

20. Flora (Alberta Nelson)

21. Howard Sprague (Jack Dodson)

22. Mabel Albertson

23. Emmett Clark (Paul Hartman)

24. Martha (Mary Lansing)

25. Roy Stoner

26. Parley Baer

27. Mayor Pike (Dick Elliott)

28. Ben Weaver

29. Howard Sprague

30. Boysingers

31. Helen Crump (Aneta Corsaut)

32. The fifth grade

33. Otis Campbell (Hal Smith)

34. Two

35. Sarah

36. Howard Morris

37. Meyers

38. Pilot

39. The Blue Bird Diner

40. Danny Thomas

Answers—Action, Thrills, and High Adventure!

1. (Yukon) King

2. *Tiki*

3. Tamba

4. (Burt) Reynolds

5. (Alexander) Mundy

6. (Chuck) Connors

7. (Captain Dan) Tempest

8. (Gentle) Ben

9. *Poseidon*

10. (Jim) Davis

11. Adamo

12. Cuffy

13. Clarence

14. (Lloyd) Bridges

15. (Martin) Milner

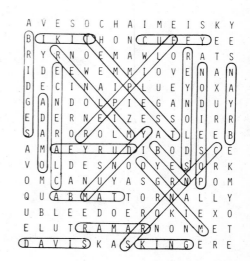

16. (Dan) Duryea

17. Mingo

18. Flipper

19. Ramar

20. (Paul) Bryan

Answers—"Andy's Gang"

1. Ed McConnell

2. Andy Devine

3. Buster Brown

4. Gunga Ram (Nino Marcel)

5. Bakore

6. Teela

7. Froggy the Gremlin, Midnight the Cat, and Squeaky the Mouse

8. Twanger

9. "N-i-i-c-e!"

10. Old Grandie

Answers—"The Avengers"

1. Patrick Macnee and Diana Rigg

2. Mrs. Catherine Gale (Honor Blackman)

3. An umbrella

4. A Bentley

5. John

6. At Number Three Stable Mews in London, England

7. Emma

8. He was believed to have been killed when the jet he was testing disintegrated

9. Tara King (Linda Thorson)

10. Mother

Courtesy Greenway Productions.

Answers—"Batman"

1. Adam West
2. Bruce Wayne
3. Burt Ward
4. Alfred Pennyworth (Alan Napier)
5. Gordon (Neil Hamilton)
6. Chief O'Hara (Stafford Repp)
7. Commissioner Gordon's daughter, Barbara
8. The Batcycle

9. The Penguin (Burgess Meredith), King Tut (Victor Buono), The Riddler (Frank Gorshin and John Astin), The Mad Hatter (David Wayne), Clock King (Walter Slezak), The Joker (Cesar Romero), The Minstrel (Van Johnson), The Bookworm (Roddy McDowall), Archer (Art Carney), Chandell (Liberace), and The Sandman (Michael Rennie)

10. George Sanders

11. The Molehill Mob

12. Tetch

13. Falseface (Malachi Throne)

14. Zelda

15. Julie Newmar, Lee Meriwether, and Eartha Kitt

16. Harriet Cooper (Madge Blake)

17. The Terrestrial or Intergalactic Scanner, The Interdigital Batsorter, The Hyperspectographic Analyzer, and The Chemo-Electric Secret Writing Detector

18. The Atomic Batpile

19. Bob Kane

20. *Detective Comics*

Answers—"Ben Casey"

1. Vince Edwards

2. Neurosurgery

3. David Zorba

4. Sam Jaffe

5. Dr. Maggie Graham

6. She was an anesthesiologist

7. Dr. Ted Hoffman (Harry Landers)

8. Niles

9. Franchot Tone

10. County General Hospital

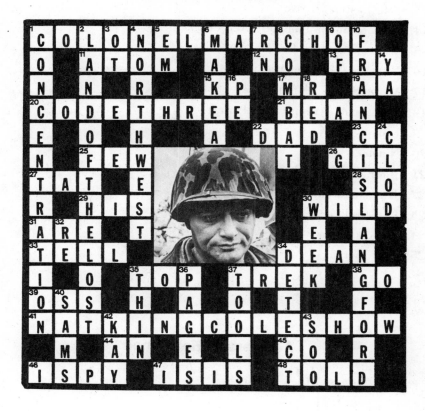

Answers—"The Beverly Hillbillies"

1. Jed Clampett
2. Daisy Moses (Irene Ryan)
3. Mr. John Brewster (Frank Wilcox), President of the O.K. Oil Company
4. Twenty-five million dollars
5. Sibly
6. Jethro Bodine
7. He had a sixth-grade education
8. Max Baer, Jr.
9. Producer Paul Henning's eighteen-year-old daughter, Linda
10. Pearl
11. Elly May (Donna Douglas)

12. Duke

13. 518 Crestview Drive

14. The Commerce Bank of Beverly Hills

15. Milton (Raymond Bailey)

16. Margaret (Margaret MacGibbon)

17. Marie (Shirry Steffin)

18. Ravenscott (Arthur Gould Porter)

19. Louis Nye

20. Nineteen years

21. Jim Backus

22. Jane Hathaway (Nancy Kulp)

23. In the billiard room

24. The cement pond

25. Flatt, Scruggs

Answers—"Bewitched"

1. Dick York and Dick Sargent

2. Elizabeth Montgomery

3. "Sam"

4. 1164 Morning Glory Circle, Westport, Connecticut

5. McMann and Tate

6. Larry Tate (David White)

7. Louise (Irene Vernon)

8. Tabitha (Erin and Diane Murphy)

9. Adam (David and Greg Lawrence)

10. Endora (Agnes Moorehead)

11. She called him "Durwood"

12. Phyllis and Frank Stevens (Mabel Albertson and Robert F. Simon)

13. Serena

14. Elizabeth Montgomery

15. Gladys Kravitz (Alice Pearce and Sandra Gould)

16. Abner (George Tobias)

17. Dr. Bombay (Bernard Fox)
18. Aunt Clara (Marion Lorne)
19. Paul Lynde
20. She wriggled her nose

Answers—"Bonanza"

1. Ben Cartwright (Lorne Greene)
2. Elizabeth (first), Inger (second), and Marie (third)
3. He served as the first mate aboard a ship
4. Virginia
5. Roy Coffee (Ray Teal)
6. The Ponderosa
7. Michael Landon
8. Dan Blocker
9. Eric
10. Adam
11. They were half-brothers
12. Candy (David Canary)
13. Little Joe
14. Griff King (Tim Matheson)
15. Hop Sing (Victor Sen Yung)

Answers—"Circus Boy"

1. A circus parade through the streets of town
2. The Flying Falcons
3. Joey
4. Noah Beery, Jr.
5. Corky
6. Mickey Braddock (Mickey Dolenz of the Monkees)
7. Bimbo

8. Pete (Guinn "Big Boy" Williams)
9. "Big Tim" Champion (Robert Lowery)
10. Mamie (wardrobe), Firpo (knife thrower), Gambino (lion tamer), Billy Stanton (trick shooter), Pop Warren (veterinarian), and Ricardo (escape artist)

Answers—"The Dick Van Dyke Show"

1. Robert "Rob" Petrie
2. Morey Amsterdam
3. Pickles (Joan Shawlee)
4. She was a showgirl
5. Rose Marie
6. Herman Glimsher (Bill Idelson)
7. Richard Deacon
8. Mel Cooley
9. Carl Reiner
10. They were brothers-in-law
11. Marge
12. Mary Tyler Moore
13. Meehan
14. Ritchie (Larry Matthews)
15. Rosebud
16. Crowder
17. He was a sergeant
18. She was a U.S.O. dancer
19. Dorothy
20. Sol Pomerantz (Allan Melvin)
21. New Rochelle, New York
22. 485 Bonnie Meadow Road
23. Jerry, Millie (Ann Morgan Guilbert)
24. He was a dentist
25. Director
26. Freddie (Peter Oliphant and David Fresco)

27. Sam and Clara

28. Stacey

29. Dick Van Dyke's real-life brother, Jerry Van Dyke

30. *High Noon*

Answers—"Dr. Kildare"

1. Richard Chamberlain

2. Lew Ayres

3. Jim

4. Raymond Massey

5. Dr. Leonard Gillespie

6. Johnson

7. Claire Trevor

8. Lawton

9. Blair

10. "Three Stars Will Shine Tonight"

Answers—Laugh-Riot

1. Mike (Brady)

2. (Hope) Lange

3. (Mrs.) O'Reilly

4. Murray (Grechner)

5. Nanny

6. (Walter) Brennan

7. (Osgood) Conklin

8. Igor

9. Florida (Evans)

10. Hubbard

11. (Ann) Sothern

12. Sue Anne (Nevins)

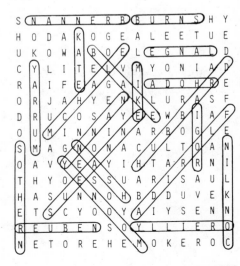

13. (Lt. Col. Henry) Blake
14. Reuben (Kincade)
15. (George) Burns
16. (Theodore J.) Mooney
17. Kate (Bradley)
18. Nash
19. (Quinton) McHale
20. Rhoda

Answers—"The Donna Reed Show"

1. Stone
2. Hilldale
3. He was a pediatrician
4. Alex
5. Carl Betz
6. Mary
7. Shelley Fabares
8. "Johnny Angel"
9. Jeff
10. Paul Petersen
11. Trisha (Patty Petersen)
12. Dr. David Kelsey
13. Bob Crane
14. Midge (Ann McCrea)
15. Bullock (Sarah Marshall and Frank Maxwell)

Answers—Crossword #2

LOVELL GEORGE M
IN ROOM SLYE LE
BEAN NUT SARGE
E RICE H ENSIGN
ROMEO JEAN H SO
A S V AWE N
CO RE DIANE
ESTER NS
BOB YOU
HOME P
RALPH CAPTAIN
AN A DARIAS IC
N ON ART BT TO
KIDS EVE C I TD
AMOS HEYJEANNIE

Answers—"Dragnet"

1. Jack Webb
2. Sergeant Ben Romero (Barton Yarborough)
3. Frank Smith
4. Ben Alexander
5. Sgt. Friday was promoted to lieutenant; Officer Smith was elevated to the rank of sergeant
6. 714
7. Harry Morgan
8. Officer Bill Gannon
9. Ann Baker (Dorothy Abbott)
10. Los Angeles

11. George Fenneman (who was also Groucho Marx's on-screen announcer)
12. Protect the innocent
13. The results of the trials of the suspects who were apprehended during the course of the episode
14. Mark VII
15. Twice

Courtesy CBS.

Answers—"The Ed Sullivan Show"

1. "Toast of the Town"
2. *The New York Daily News*
3. The Toastettes
4. They all appeared on the first Sullivan show, broadcast June 20, 1948
5. Meade

Courtesy CBS.

6. Ray Bloch

7. Dean Martin, Jerry Lewis

8. Topo Gigio

9. Louis Mouse

10. Wayne and Shuster

11. Elvis Presley

12. Margaret Truman, daughter of President Harry S. Truman

13. The Beatles

14. Sylvia

15. "Stand up and take a bow!"

Answers—"Father Knows Best"

1. Jim Anderson

2. Robert Young

3. He was an insurance salesman

4. Margaret

5. Betty (Elinor Donahue)

6. "Princess"

7. Bud (Billy Gray)

8. Kathy (Lauren Chapin)

9. "Kitten"

10. Springfield

Answers—"The Flintstones"

1. Bedrock

2. Slate Rock Gravel Company

3. George Slate

4. His dinner

5. Dino

6. Mel Blanc

7. Wilma

8. Flaghoople

9. Bowling

10. Foot

11. Bea Benaderet (Gerry Johnson later replaced Miss Benaderet as Betty Rubble's voice)

12. Pebbles

13. He was the strongest baby in the world

14. Bamm Bamm was abandoned on the Rubbles' doorstep as a baby

15. Hoppy

16. Water Buffaloes

17. *The Bedrock Daily Slate*

18. Alan Reed (Fred Flintstone) and Mel Blanc (Barney Rubble)

19. Gazoo

20. Harvey Korman

© 1978 Hanna-Barbera Productions, Inc.

Answers—And Away We Go!

1. (Art) Linkletter
2. (Red) Barber
3. (Mitch) Miller
4. (Garry) Moore
5. (Alan) Funt
6. Joe
7. (Jimmy) Durante

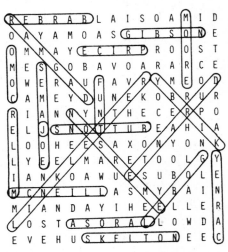

8. (Dennis) James
9. Dagmar
10. (George) Gobel
11. (Julius) LaRosa
12. (Art) Carney
13. (Perry) Como
14. (Red) Skelton
15. (Red) Buttons
16. (Durwood) Kirby
17. (Roger) Price
18. (Faye) Emerson
19. (Henry) Gibson
20. (Don) McNeill

Answers—"The Fugitive"

1. David Janssen
2. Helen (Diane Brewster)
3. Indiana
4. A train derailment
5. Lieutenant Phillip Gerard (Barry Morse)
6. Because Kimble had escaped from Gerard's custody
7. Marie Gerard (Barbara Rush)
8. Black hair dye
9. He exhibited a nervous facial twitch
10. Frank Johnson
11. Bill Raisch
12. Donna (Jacqueline Scott)
13. Gerard handed Kimble his gun and told him to go after the one-armed man
14. J. D. Stone
15. William Conrad

Courtesy Worldvision Enterprises, Inc.

Answers—"Fury"

1. Joey (Bobby Diamond)
2. Jim
3. Peter Graves
4. Helen Watkins
5. Pete (William Fawcett)
6. Broken Wheel
7. Twin Forks
8. Lucky

9. Thunder

10. Gypsy

Answers—"The Gene Autry Show"

1. Champion
2. He played himself
3. "Back in the Saddle Again"
4. Pat Buttram
5. Roy Rogers
6. The Melody Ranch
7. Wrigley's Gum
8. A
9. "Rudolph the Red-Nosed Reindeer"
10. California Angels

Answers—Photo Quiz #1

1. Hugh O'Brian
2. Astro
3. Barnabas Collins (Jonathan Frid)
4. Left to right: Loco Jones (Barbara Eden), Michele Page (Merry Anders), and Greta Lindquist (Lori Nelson)
5. "Flipper"
6. Johnny Corso
7. Wileyville
8. Jeff Donnell
9. Snidely Whiplash
10. Don Jagger

Answers—"Get Smart"

1. Don Adams
2. C.O.N.T.R.O.L.
3. He stepped inside a phone booth, dialed a number, and dropped through the floor of the booth into his spy agency's headquarters
4. 123 Main Street, Washington, D.C.
5. 86
6. 99
7. "Chief" (Edward Platt)
8. Thaddeus
9. Larrabee (Robert Knowles)
10. Harold Clark
11. K.A.O.S.
12. Conrad Siegfried (Bernie Kopell)
13. Starker (King Moody)
14. 13
15. Hymie
16. Fang
17. It was the same as his C.O.N.T.R.O.L. number—86
18. Admiral Harold Harmon Hargrade (William Schallert)
19. Would you believe his shoe?
20. The pilot episode was broadcast in black-and-white. All other episodes were in color

Answers—Crossword #3

Answers—"Gilligan's Island"

1. The S.S. *Minnow*
2. Hawaii
3. Three
4. Alan Hale, Jr.
5. Jonas Grumby
6. Ginger Grant
7. Tina Louise
8. Mary Ann Summers (Dawn Wells)
9. Kansas
10. Thurston Howell III
11. Jim Backus

12. Lovey (Natalie Schafer)

13. He didn't teach in college. He was a high school science teacher

14. Roy Hinkley (Russell Johnson)

15. Bob Denver

Courtesy CBS.

Answers—"Gunsmoke"

1. John Wayne

2. James Arness

3. *The Thing*

4. Peter Graves

5. Arvo Ojala

6. A bartender in the Long Branch Saloon

7. Marshal

8. Long Branch
9. Sam (Glenn Strange)
10. Dennis Weaver
11. Ken Curtis
12. Ruth
13. Galen Adams
14. Pat Hingle
15. Dr. John Chapman
16. Burt Reynolds
17. Quint Asper
18. Newly O'Brien (Buck Taylor)
19. Ma Smalley (Sarah Selby)
20. The series expanded from a half-hour to a full-hour telecast

Answers—"Have Gun, Will Travel"

1. Paladin
2. Richard Boone
3. The white chess knight, a Paladin
4. Belt
5. Carlton
6. Hey Boy (Kam Tong)
7. Hey Girl (Lisa Lu)
8. San Francisco
9. "Have Gun Will Travel. Wire Paladin. San Francisco."
10. Johnny Western

Answers—Calling All Cars!

1. (Lee) Marvin
2. Mother's
3. (Pete) Malloy

4. Intertect

5. "Naked City"

6. (Paul) Garrett

7. Kato

8. (Louis) Jourdan

9. (Reed) Hadley

10. (Sebastian) Cabot

11. Asta

12. Daphne (deWitt Dutton)

13. (Robert) Stack

14. (Martin) Kane

15. (Broderick) Crawford

16. (Dan) Briggs

17. (Beverly) Garland

18. Preston

19. (Amos) Burke

20. (Robert) Taylor

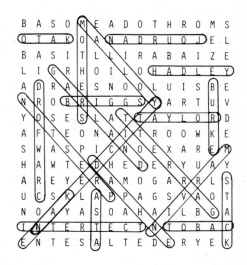

Answers—"Hawaiian Eye"

1. Tom Lopaka (Robert Conrad), Gregg MacKenzie (Grant Williams), and Tracy Steele (Anthony Eisley)

2. Hawaiian Village

3. Cricket Blake

4. Connie Stevens

5. The Arthur Lyman Band

6. Kim (Poncie Ponce)

7. Phillip Barton

8. Troy Donahue

9. Lois Lorey

10. Lt. Danny Quon (Mel Prestidge) and Moke (Doug Mosserman)

Answers—"Hazel"

1. Shirley Booth
2. Burke
3. Don DeFore
4. Harry Noll (Lauren Gilbert)
5. Miss Scott (Molly Dodd)
6. Dorothy (Whitney Blake)
7. Interior decorating
8. Harold (Bobby Buntrock)
9. Hazel called Mr. Baxter "Mr. B.," Mrs. Baxter "Missy," and Harold "Sport"
10. Smiley
11. 123 Marshall Road
12. Herbert and Harriet Johnson (Donald Foster and Norma Varlen)
13. Griffin (Howard Smith)
14. Harvey
15. His mother
16. Mitch Brady (Dub Taylor)
17. The Checkerboard Cab Company
18. Rosie (Maudie Prickett)
19. Dr. Craig
20. Sunshine
21. Bowler
22. Barney Hatfield (Robert B. Williams)
23. Deirdre (Cathy Lewis)
24. Harry (Robert P. Lieb)
25. Eddie Burke (John Washbrook)
26. Mamie
27. To the Middle East
28. Barbara
29. Lynn Borden
30. Susie (Julia Benjamin)

Answers—"Hogan's Heroes"

1. Stalag 13
2. Robert (Bob Crane)
3. The U.S. Air Force
4. "Papa Bear"
5. Colonel Wilhelm Klink (Werner Klemperer)
6. He was a bookkeeper
7. Sergeant Hans Schultz (John Banner)
8. A toy company
9. Helga (Cynthia Lynn) in early episodes; Hilda (Sigrid Valdis) in later episodes
10. None
11. Richard Dawson
12. Louis
13. He was the cook
14. Sgt. Andrew Carter (Larry Hovis)
15. Corporal James Kinchloe (Kenneth Washington)
16. When they banged on one of the top bunks, the bottom bunk would open up, revealing a trap door and ladder leading down into the underground tunnel
17. Under a doghouse in the kennel
18. A tree stump
19. In a picture of Adolph Hitler that was hanging on the wall
20. A coffeepot lid

Answers—"The Honeymooners"

1. Pert Kelton
2. Kramden
3. Two
4. 328 Chauncey Street
5. Mr. Johnson
6. Alice
7. Gibson

8. Audrey Meadows

9. Marshall

10. Mr. Monahan

11. 225 River Street

12. Norton

13. Art Carney

14. Trixie

15. In the sewer

16. Raccoon

17. Morris Fink

18. Right in the kisser

19. To the moon

20. You're the greatest

Answers—Crossword #4

```
R I C H A R D C R E N N A   A        H
O N   A L   R A I N E S       D A    A
B A N D S T A N D     V               V
I R A     O K     H I G H             E
N A P S   M E R R I L L           A   G
    Y E S             L E E        U
        T D           E N D        N
L I Z   A N           N E W W
U A     N N               N E W
K E N               B         B A    
E V E L Y N   A R N E S S         Y
    E   A   O B R I E N       L A
    I   U   L O E B       N O A H S   S
D O U G L A S         H Y       D     E
A N   H A N S     U S         T E L E
```

Answers—"Hopalong Cassidy"

1. William Boyd
2. "Hoppy"
3. Topper
4. White
5. Gabby Hayes
6. Red Connors
7. Lucky (Russell Hayden) and California (Andy Clyde)
8. Bar 20
9. Crescent City
10. Clarence E. Mulford

Answers—"The Howdy Doody Show"

1. "Puppet Playhouse"
2. Buffalo Bob Smith
3. Texas
4. Bob Smith
5. Cornelius J. "Corny" Cobb
6. Hornblow
7. By honking "yes" and "no" with an auto horn
8. Bob Keeshan, who stars as Captain Kangaroo
9. Pesky the Evil Clown
10. The Flubadub
11. Meatballs and spaghetti
12. Dilly Dally
13. Phineas T. Bluster
14. Petey
15. Princess Summer-Fall-Winter-Spring (Judy Tyler) and Chief Thunderthud (Bill Lecornec)
16. "Kowabunga!"
17. Double Doody
18. Mambo

19. Alene Dalton

20. Heidi

21. Captain Scuttlebutt

22. Willie

23. The Doodyville Doodlers

24. Peppi Mint

25. Peanut

Answers—"I Dream of Jeannie"

1. Major Anthony Nelson (Larry Hagman)

2. 2,000

3. Barbara Eden

4. Baghdad

5. The Blue Djin

6. Michael Ansara

7. Melissa (Karen Sharpe)

8. Roger Healy

9. She folded her arms and blinked her eyes

10. Two—Majors Nelson and Healy

11. 1020 Palm Drive, Cocoa Beach, Florida

12. Alfred Bellows (Hayden Rourke)

13. Amanda

14. General Martin Peterson (Barton MacLane)

15. Hadji (Abraham Safaer)

16. Harold

17. Jeannie II (Barbara Eden)

18. Habib (Ted Cassidy)

19. Gin Gin

20. Spring Byington

Answers—"I Love Lucy"

1. Lucy Ricardo
2. MacGillicuddy
3. Ricky
4. Desi Arnaz
5. The Tropicana
6. Babalu
7. *TV Guide*
8. Little Ricky (Richard Keith)
9. 623 East 68th Street, New York City (Apartment 3-B)
10. Trumble (Elizabeth Patterson)
11. Ethel, Fred
12. Frawley, Vance
13. They were vaudeville entertainers
14. Alberto (George Trevino)
15. *Don Juan*

Answers—Say, Kids! What Time Is It?

1. Capt. Midnight
2. Rusty
3. Mr. Wizard
4. (Paul) Tripp
5. (Miss) Frances
6. (Wally) Cox
7. Ready
8. (Mary) Hartline
9. Baba Looey
10. Tagg
11. (Fran) Allison
12. (Rod) Brown
13. (Shari) Lewis
14. Rocky

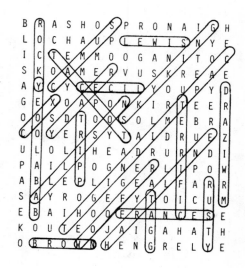

15. (Poison) Sumac
16. Top Cat
17. Woofer
18. Cecil
19. Sky King
20. (Tom) Terrific

Answers—"The Jack Benny Show"

1. Rochester (Eddie Anderson)
2. Mel Blanc
3. A Maxwell
4. Frank Nelson
5. In an underground vault
6. It was unlisted
7. Marilyn Monroe
8. The Sportsmen
9. Gertrude
10. Dennis Day and Rochester
11. Mel Blanc
12. Love in Bloom
13. Don Wilson
14. Thirty-nine
15. J-E-L-L-O!

Answers—"Lassie"

1. Tommy Rettig
2. Ellen (Jan Clayton)
3. Calverton
4. He inherited her from a neighbor who had passed away
5. Brockway (Donald Keeler)

6. Sylvester

7. Pokey

8. Matt Brockway (Paul Mavey)

9. Doc Frank Weaver (Arthur Space)

10. Domino

11. Jenny

12. Dr. Stuart (Dayton Lummis)

13. Ruth, Paul (Jon Shepodd)

14. Cloris Leachman

15. Timmy (Jon Provost)

16. Uncle Petrie (George Chandler)

17. Cully (Andy Clyde)

18. Ranger Corey Stuart (Robert Bray)

19. Rudd Weatherwax

20. Campbell's Soups

Answers—"Leave It to Beaver"

1. Jerry Mathers

2. Theodore

3. June and Ward

4. Tony Dow

5. Mayfield

6. Larry Mundello (Rusty Stevens)

7. Judy Hensler (Jeri Weil)

8. Landers (Sue Randall)

9. Mrs. Rayburn (Doris Packer)

10. Whitney (Stanley Fafara)

11. Gus (Burt Mustin)

12. Eddie Haskell (Ken Osmond)

13. Lumpy (Frank Bank)

14. Richard Deacon

15. Fred

Answers—And Here's Your Host . . .

1. (Mike) Stokey
2. (Jack) Bailey
3. (Jack) Narz
4. (Merv) Griffin
5. (Ralph) Story
6. (Bud) Collyer
7. (Herb) Shriner
8. (Bill) Cullen
9. (Edgar) Bergen
10. (Jan) Murray
11. (Art) James
12. (Garry) Moore
13. (Gene) Rayburn
14. (Bert) Parks
15. (Bill) Leyden
16. (Peter) Donald
17. (John) Daly
18. (Warren) Hull
19. (George) de Witt
20. (Jack) Barry

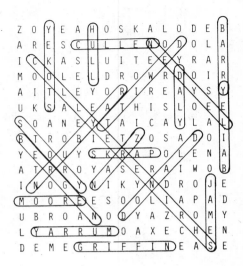

Answers—"The Life of Riley"

1. William Bendix
2. Blue View
3. Hammock
4. Cunningham
5. He was a riveter
6. Hawkins
7. Otto Schmidlap (Henry Kulky)
8. Peg
9. Babs (Lugene Sanders) and Junior (Wesley Morgan)

10. Jim (Tom D' Andrea) and Honeybee (Gloria Blondell)
11. Jimsey
12. Egbert (Gregory Marshall)
13. Los Angeles
14. Brooklyn Patriots of Los Angeles
15. Calvin and Belle Dudley (George O'Hanlon and Florence Sundstrom)
16. Martin Milner
17. Chester
18. Waldo Binny (Sterling Holloway)
19. What a revoltin' development this is!
20. Jackie Gleason and Rosemary DeCamp

Answers—"The Lone Ranger"

1. John Reid
2. John Hart
3. Clayton Moore
4. Silver
5. Tonto
6. He was a Mohawk Indian
7. Scout
8. Kemo sabe
9. Silver
10. Hi-yo, Silver! Away!

Answers—"Love That Bob"

1. Bob Collins
2. Margaret and Chuck MacDonald (Rosemary DeCamp and Dwayne Hickman)
3. Paul Fonda (Lyle Talbot)
4. Francine Williams (Diane Jergens)

5. Charmaine "Schultzy" Schultz (Ann B. Davis)
6. Frank Crenshaw (Dick Wesson)
7. Josh Collins
8. Joplin, Missouri
9. Bob Cummings
10. "Old Jenny"
11. He was a photographer
12. Shirley Swanson
13. Harvey Helm (King Donavon)
14. Kay Michael (Lola Albright)
15. Pamela Livingston

Answers—"Make Room for Daddy"

1. Williams
2. Rusty (Rusty Hamer) and Terry (Sherry Jackson, later Penney Parker)
3. 505 East 50th Street (Apartment 542), New York City
4. Laddie
5. Jean Hagen
6. Kathy (Marjorie Lord)
7. Daly
8. She was a nurse
9. Linda
10. Jesse Leeds (Jesse White)
11. Ben "Benny" Lessy
12. Tonoose
13. Hans Conreid
14. Toledo, Ohio
15. Louise (Amanda Randolph)
16. The Copa
17. Sid Melton
18. Bunny
19. Mr. Heckendorn
20. Gale Gordon

21. Mr. Svenson (John Qualen)
22. Bill Dana
23. He was the elevator operator
24. Harry Ruby
25. Sheldon Leonard
26. Gina Minelli
27. Annette Funicello
28. Pat Hannigan
29. Pat Harrington, Jr.
30. Golf pro Guido Panzini

Answers—Crossword #5

ROCKY DANGERMAN
O BE BAT OR DA
DS LEAN MAC AM
BULLWINKLE H ME
RB Y NYC REED
O B C REEL L
W I A A I
NIGHT BURKE
V AS AS I
JEAN CH ITS F
O SEVEN H T F
EB GI B TEACH
YOGI C COOL HAT
NA A I ZOO NO
RESTLESS TRICK

Answers—"The Man from U.N.C.L.E."

1. United Network Command for Law Enforcement
2. Napoleon Solo
3. Agent 11
4. Illya N. Kuryakin
5. Leo G. Carroll
6. Alexander
7. A tailor shop
8. Mr. Del Floria (Mario Siletti)
9. New York City
10. Sarah (Leigh Chapman)
11. Heather McNab (May Heatherly)
12. Communications
13. In a pencil
14. T.H.R.U.S.H.
15. "The Girl from U.N.C.L.E."

Answers—"The Many Loves of Dobie Gillis"

1. Dwayne Hickman
2. They owned a grocery store
3. 285 Norwood Street
4. Central City
5. Herbert T. Gillis (Frank Faylen)
6. The "Good Conduct" Medal
7. Winifred "Winnie" Gillis (Florida Friebus)
8. Maynard G. Krebs (Bob Denver)
9. "You rang?"
10. Watching old buildings being torn down
11. *The Monster That Devoured Cleveland*
12. Blonde
13. Brown
14. Tuesday Weld

15. Milton Armitage
16. Warren Beatty
17. Clarice (Doris Packer)
18. Chatsworth Osborne, Jr. (Steve Franken)
19. Davey
20. Darryl Hickman, Dwayne's brother
21. Zelda Gilroy (Sheila James)
22. William Schallert
23. Charlie Wong (John Lee)
24. Lt. Merriweather (Richard Claire)
25. Max Shulman

Answers—Photo Quiz #2

1. Six hundred pounds
2. Ralph Edwards
3. Left to right: Blabber, Snooper, Doggie Daddy, Augie Doggie, Quick Draw McGraw (the series' star), and Baba Looey
4. Duncan Renaldo and Leo Carillo
5. John Newland
6. David Vincent (Roy Thinnes)
7. The San Fernando Valley
8. Richard Simmons
9. The *Leakin' Lena*
10. Nick Adams

Answers—"Maverick"

1. Luck, gambling
2. Bret
3. Beauregard Maverick
4. Samantha Crawford
5. Bart Maverick (Jack Kelly)

6. Richard Long

7. Roger Moore

8. Brent (Robert Colbert)

9. Jim Buckley

10. Efrem Zimbalist, Jr.

Answers—Hometown Folks

1. New Hope
2. Tucson
3. Bronx
4. Palm Springs
5. Grover City
6. New York (City)
7. San Diego
8. Los Angeles
9. Beverly Hills
10. Bryant Park
11. Chicago
12. Pelham
13. Rossmore
14. Huberie
15. Monterey
16. Santa Fe
17. Jackson
18. San Juan
19. Velardi
20. London

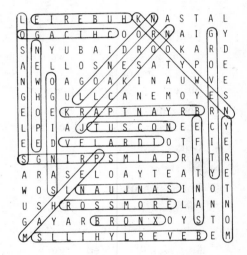

Answers—"The Mickey Mouse Club"

1. Twenty-four (twelve girls, twelve boys)
2. Jimmy Dodd

3. Roy Williams

4. Annette Funicello

5. Bobby Burgess

6. Music, Roundup, Star, Happen

7. "Spin and Marty"

8. Frank and Joe Hardy—"The Hardy Boys"

9. Darlene Gillespie, as Corky Brady

10. Cliff "Ukulele Ike" Edwards

Answers—"The Millionaire"

1. John Beresford Tipton

2. Tipton was played by a well-known radio actor who disguised his voice to keep his identity secret. This was done in an attempt to make the mythical billionaire character appear more believable to the viewing audience

3. The name was a composite of producer Don Fedderson's home town, his wife's home town, and his lawyer's first name

4. Ivory chess pieces

5. Silverstone

6. Michael Anthony

7. Gotham City Trust and Savings

8. If he revealed the source of his newfound wealth

9. Mrs. Don (Tido) Fedderson appeared in every episode of the series. When not appearing in person, she was seen in a photograph, on a calendar, etc.

10. "If You Had a Million"

Answers—"Mr. Ed"

1. A palomino

2. Post (Alan Young and Connie Hines)

3. He was left to him by the previous owner of his house

4. He was an architect

5. No one

6. Chuck (Ricki Starr)
7. Roger and Kay Addison (Larry Keating and Edna Skinner)
8. Lady Linda
9. Gordon and Winnie Kirkwood (Leon Ames and Florence MacMichael)
10. Rocky Layne

Answers—"Mr. Peepers"

1. Wally Cox
2. Science
3. Jefferson City Junior High School
4. Robinson
5. Nancy Remington
6. Harvey Weskit—"Wes"
7. Tony Randall
8. Mrs. Gurney
9. Mr. Bascomb (George Clark)
10. Jack Warden

Answers—Crossword #6

The crossword grid reads:

M	O	T	H	E	R	S		S	E	A	R	C	H
I		H	E		A	T		T	A	K	E		O	F
C	L	A	Y		G	A	B	O	R		P	A	U	L
H	O	T		G		R	E	N	N	I	E		S	E
A	N	S	W	E	R		N	E		N	A	K	E	D
E			A							T	O			
L	A	R	R	Y				A		J	A	N		
C	H	A	D					C	H	A	S	E		
O		I						E		K			W	
L	I	N	C								B			
E	M	E	R	S	O	N		S	O	L	D	I	E	R
	Y	E	O	M	E	N			R		R		S	O
I	S		A		A	O			P	A	T	T	Y	
S	H	A	T	N	E	R		P	L	O	W			A
H	E	R	E		D	S		L	A	W		S	A	L

Answers—"My Favorite Martian"

1. Ray Walston
2. Martin
3. He was an anthropologist specializing in the study of Earth
4. Bill Bixby
5. Newspaper reporter
6. "What are you waiting for me to say—take me to your leader?"
7. Lorelei Brown (Pamela Britton)
8. Bill Brennan
9. A molecular reassembler
10. He pointed his finger at the object to be levitated and guided its movement

216

Answers—"My Little Margie"

1. The Carlton Arms Hotel
2. Apartment 10-A
3. Vern
4. Charles Farrell
5. Real estate
6. Honeywell and Todd
7. He was vice-president
8. George Honeywell (Clarence Kolb)
9. Roberta Townsend (Hillary Brooke)
10. Gale Storm
11. Albright
12. Twenty-one years old
13. Freddie Wilson (Don Hayden)
14. Mrs. Odettes (Gertrude Hoffman)
15. Charlie (Willie Best)

Answers—"The People's Choice"

1. Jackie Cooper
2. He was a city councilman
3. New
4. Gus (Margaret Irving)
5. Mandy Peoples (Patricia Breslin)
6. Rollo (Dick Wesson)
7. Roger Crutcher (John Stephenson)
8. Pierre (Leonid Kinskey)
9. Cleo
10. Mary Jane Croft

Answers—Dramatic Pause

1. (George C.) Scott
2. (Adolph) Menjou
3. (Mike) Kovac
4. Pamela
5. April (Dancer)
6. Kelly (Robinson)
7. Six
8. (Albert) Vane
9. (Dr. Ted) Stuart
10. (Harry) Lime
11. (Dr. Theodore) Bassett
12. Pinky (Pinkham)
13. (Jim) McKay
14. (Dr. Paul) Lochner
15. Frieda (Krause)
16. (Dr. Steve) Kiley
17. (Boris) Karloff
18. O'Henry
19. (William) Lundigan
20. (Rick) Jason

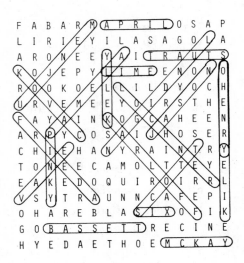

Answers—"Perry Mason"

1. Raymond Burr
2. Los Angeles, California
3. Della Street
4. Gertie Lade (Connie Cezon)
5. Paul Drake
6. William Hopper
7. Hamilton Burger (William Talman)
8. Lieutenant Tragg
9. Arthur

Courtesy CBS.

10. Anderson
11. Lt. Steve Drumm (Richard Anderson)
12. Bette Davis
13. None
14. Erle Stanley Gardner
15. One

Answers—"Rawhide"

1. San Antonio, Texas
2. Sedalia, Missouri
3. Three thousand
4. Gil Favor

5. Eric Fleming

6. Clint Eastwood

7. Wishbone

8. Mushy

9. Sheb Wooley

10. Frankie Laine

Answers—"The Rifleman"

1. Lucas McCain

2. The Boston Celtics

3. A 44-40 Winchester

4. Mark

5. Johnny Crawford

6. North Fork

7. Micah Torrance (Paul Fix)

8. Scott (Joan Taylor)

9. Miss Adele Adams (Patricia Barry)

10. Lou Mallory (Patricia Blair)

Courtesy Four Star Entertainment Corporation.

Answers—"The Roy Rogers Show"

1. Dale Evans
2. Buttercup
3. Trigger
4. Bullet
5. Pat Brady
6. He worked as a short-order cook in Roy's restaurant
7. Nellybelle
8. Aloysius
9. The Double R Bar Ranch
10. Happy Trails to You

Answers—Crossword #7

```
D O O D L E S W E A V E R   S
O   A   P T V   I M     M E
R A I N S   A   E D   V I C
I     G O I N G   H E C   L R
S I R E N   D O C C O R K L E
D O O R S           O R   T
A   M           S W A T
Y E A R S       M   F O R
  G N   R       O   T O D
D O T T O       T H
U   I   G I G   O H E N R Y
P E C K S   M A C N E E   O
O   I T   B A E R   S I R
N E L S O N   O N   S T A C K
T   S P E A R     A M E S
```

221

Answers—"77 Sunset Strip"

1. Efrem Zimbalist, Jr.
2. Jeff Spencer
3. Ann-Margret
4. Kookie
5. "Kookie, Kookie (Lend Me Your Comb)"
6. A Model T Ford
7. Dino's Lodge
8. Gerald Lloyd Kookson III
9 He became a full-fledged investigator with the 77 Sunset Strip firm
10. J. R. Hale (Robert Logan)
11. Roscoe
12. Louie Quinn
13. Suzanne Fabray (Jacqueline Beer)
14. A telephone-answering service
15. "Bourbon Street Beat"
16. Richard Long
17. Hannah
18. Stuart Bailey
19. Lt. Gilmore (Byron Keith)
20. Stuart Bailey

Answers—"The $64,000 Question"

1. Hal March
2. Lynn Dollar
3. IBM computer
4. Cadillac convertible
5. Isolation booths
6. Children's stories
7. Dr. Joyce Brothers
8. Robert Strom
9. Mrs. Myrt Power

10. Billy Pearson
11. Gino Prato
12. Terry Nadler
13. Dr. Bergen Evans
14. Revlon
15. Barbara Britton

Answers—Who Was That Masked Man?

1. Pancho
2. Champion
3. Bodie
4. (Seth) Adams
5. (Steve) McQueen
6. El Toro
7. Bat (Masterson)
8. Victoria (Barkley)
9. (Jason) McCord
10. (Dick) Powell
11. (Jim) Hardie
12. Billy (the Kid)
13. (Joel) McCrea
14. Zorro
15. (Vint) Bonner
16. Flicka
17. (Judge Roy) Bean
18. (Jim) Redigo
19. Cannon
20. (Hugh) O'Brian

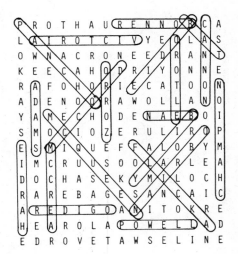

Answers—"Star Trek"

1. Five years
2. The 23rd century
3. Captain James T. Kirk (William Shatner)
4. The U.S.S. *Enterprise*
5. NCC 1701
6. *Galileo*
7. Captain Christopher Pike (Jeffrey Hunter)
8. Mr. Spock (Leonard Nimoy)
9. Amanda (Jane Wyatt)
10. To the area on top of the right shoulder, near the base of the neck
11. Leonard McCoy (De Forest Kelley)
12. "Bones"
13. Mr. Spock
14. Lieutenant Uhura (Nichelle Nichols)
15. "Scotty"—Montgomery Scott (James Doohan)
16. Jeffries
17. Pavla Chekov (Walter Koenig)
18. Mr. Sulu (George Takei)
19. Mr. Spock
20. Warp
21. Phasers
22. Sensors
23. Tricorder
24. The Communicator
25. Trekkies

Answers—"The Steve Allen Show"

1. "The Ed Sullivan Show"
2. Gene Rayburn
3. Steve Lawrence and Eydie Gorme
4. Don Knotts

5. "Nope!"

6. Louis Nye

7. "Hi ho, Steverino!"

8. His name

9. Skitch Henderson

10. Bill Dana

Answers—"Texaco Star Theater"

1. Tuesday
2. Television
3. "I'll give you a shot in the head!"
4. Uncle
5. Million
6. Arnold Stang
7. Ruth Gilbert
8. Max
9. "I'll tell ya what I'm gonna do!"
10. Jimmy Nelson, Danny O'Day

Answers—Crossword #8

JOANNEWORLEY SO
E RYAN U ODETTA
TATES IT X LOOK
S HIDE MAN
OPEN CARGO SEA
NAME PAT M
SOMES IS TO
LADD C LES
RO KILL
OZZIE N LT
OZARK CINDY A A
MINE JAFFE STAR
EFREM LATE FG
IT U APE TEAM E
TOMLIN CAHN ART

Answers—"The Today Show"

1. Dave Garroway
2. Peace
3. Charles Van Doren
4. Betsy Palmer
5. Jack Lescoulie
6. Frank Blair
7. J. Fred Muggs
8. He sued the show's host, Dave Garroway, and the NBC network for $500,000—claiming defamation of character
9. The Manhattan early-risers stood on the sidewalk waving through large glass windows as the television camera panned across them
10. Hugh Downs

Answers—"Topper"

1. Marion, George
2. Leo G. Carroll
3. Cosmo
4. Neil
5. A Saint Bernard
6. They were buried in a snow avalanche while on a skiing trip
7. Their fifth anniversary
8. The National Security Bank
9. He was vice-president
10. Schuyler (Thurston Hall)
11. New York City
12. Katie (Kathleen Freeman)
13. Henrietta
14. Only Topper could see and hear them
15. The Kirbys were the former owners of the Topper home

Answers—"What's My Line?"

1. Dorothy Kilgallen, Ex-New Jersey Governor Harold Hoffman, poet Louis Untermeyer, and Dr. Richard Hoffman
2. John Daly
3. Charles
4. Arlene Francis
5. Bennett Cerf, Dorothy Kilgallen
6. A hat-check girl
7. They had to sign in
8. Mystery
9. Ex-Yankee shortstop Phil Rizzuto
10. Goodson, Todman

Answers—More Canned Laughter

1. Lurch
2. (Mr.) Quigley
3. (Inger) Stevens
4. Goldbergs
5. Mike
6. (Dr. Morton) Chegley
7. (Captain Daniel) Gregg
8. (Gunther) Toody
9. (Arthur) Lake
10. Beulah
11. Elsie
12. Lou Anne (Poovie)
13. (Jackie) Cooper
14. Paula (Hollister)
15. Kelly (Gregg)
16. Porter
17. Day
18. (Mrs.) Livingston
19. (Ann) Sothern
20. Ann Marie

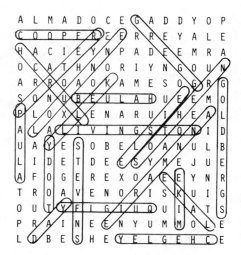

Answers—"You Bet Your Life"

1. "Say the secret word and you win a hundred dollars"
2. A duck
3. Marilyn Burtis
4. One hundred dollars
5. One thousand dollars
6. Two
7. Ten thousand dollars
8. Who is buried in Grant's Tomb?
9. Groucho sent you
10. George Fenneman

Answers—"You'll Never Get Rich"

1. Phil Silvers
2. Fort Baxter
3. Roseville, Kansas
4. Motor pool
5. Colonel John T. Hall (Paul Ford)
6. Nell (Hope Sansberry)
7. Tige Andrews
8. Barbarella (Harvey Lembeck)
9. Duane Doberman (Maurice Gosfield)
10. Joan Hogan
11. Rupert Ritzik
12. Emma (Beatrice Pons)
13. Zippy
14. Camel
15. Nat Hiken

Answers—Photo Quiz #3

1. "Big Town"
2. Sweet Polly Purebred
3. Gail Davis
4. Rick Jason
5. Wladziu Valentino Liberace
6. Snagglepuss
7. Kato (Bruce Lee)
8. Richard Webb
9. Thomas Mitchell
10. Charles Bronson